JESUS
TODAY

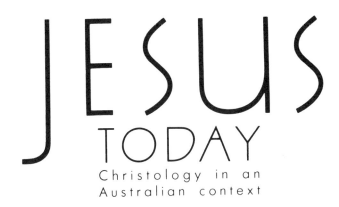

JESUS
TODAY
Christology in an
Australian context

Gerald O'Collins, SJ

Paulist Press
New York • Mahwah

Published by DOVE COMMUNICATIONS
60-64 Railway Road, Blackburn, Victoria 3130
Telephone (03) 877 1333

First published in the United States by
PAULIST PRESS
997 Macarthur Boulevard, Mahwah, NJ 07430

Designed by Mary Goodburn
Typeset in 11½ on 12½ Sabon by Bookset, North Melbourne
Printed in Australia

Cover illustrations from the etching 'Transfiguration'
by Marvin Hayes, from GOD'S IMAGES.
Copyright © 1977 by Oxmoor House, Inc.
Reproduced by permission of the publisher.

National Library of Australia
Cataloguing-in-Publication data:
O'Collins, Gerald, 1931-
    Jesus today.
    ISBN 0 85924 431 8.

    1. Jesus Christ — Person and offices. I. Title.
232

ISBN: 0-8091-2804-7

CONTENTS

PREFACE

Talking about God is always a losing battle. How can we possibly get this topic into proper perspective? From beginning to end we run the risk of re-inventing the infinite God in our own finite image and likeness.

To write and speak about Jesus Christ, the Son of God and Saviour of the world, can appear slightly less daunting. After all, his humanity and earthly history line him up with us. Nevertheless, any systematic reflection on him will always betray our personal experience of him and attitude towards him. Which of us dare boast that he or she has fully experienced Jesus and has a satisfactory attitude towards him? Rather, we can only apply to ourselves his question to Philip: 'Have I been with you so long, and yet you do not know me?' (John 14:9).

After these disclaimers, let me settle for what I can do. In this book I set out first to explore certain basic components for any serious study of Jesus Christ: some account of the human condition, the use of historical data (Chapter 1), the paschal mystery as starting-point and centre, and the challenge of communicating not merely our common Christian beliefs about Jesus, but also his meaningful presence (Chapter 2).

Once or twice in his novels, when he wanted to round things off, Charles Dickens despatched some character out to Australia. For nearly two hundred years that island-continent has often been a dumping ground for people and ideas that were not succeeding elsewhere. Before he takes off for Australia, the alcoholic hero of the film *Educating Rita* remarks: 'I've heard it's a paradise for the likes of me.' Can that paradise in the South Seas come up with any genuinely local answers to the question, 'Who do you say that I am?' If not, Australians will continue to respond only to the prior question: 'Who do Europeans, North Americans, Latin Americans, Africans and Asians say that I am?' Hence Chapter 3 sketches some elements for an Australian-style Christology. In my experience, to speak of theology 'Down Under' usually evokes a look of surprise or disbelief. Yet in Australia as elsewhere the attempt should be made to think locally. Chapter 3 could also illustrate something of what a consciously local theology might look like.

Since Chapter 1 argues for the centrality of the paschal mystery, Chapter 4 will take up some contemporary issues about the resurrection. The book ends with some suggestions for interpreting Jesus as Saviour of the world and Son of God.

This work came into being as a result of an invitation to deliver the 1985 'Anniversary Lectures', marking the seventy-fifth birthday of the Melbourne College of Divinity. I want to express my sincere thanks to the Standing Committee of the College and its Dean, Dr John Henley, for honouring me with this invitation and for efficiently taking care of all the arrangements. I wish also to acknowledge gratefully the part Dove Communications played in making this book possible. For years some dear friends, such as John Begley, Archbishop Peter Carnley, William Dalton, Archbishop Sir Frank Little, Helen Lombard, Adrian Lyons, Davis and Jean McCaughey Charles O'Mahoney, Patrick O'Sullivan, Noel Ryan, Peter Steele, Bishop Bernard Wallace and John Wilcken have encouraged me to think about Christology in an Australian context. My warm thanks go to them, and to Leslie Wearne, who once again has superbly typed a manuscript for me.

I dedicate this book with much love to nineteen persons who have greatly blessed and enriched my life, my nephews and nieces.

The Gregorian University   *Gerald O'Collins, SJ*
Rome

1
INTERPRETING
JESUS
TODAY

What do we expect from any serious and systematic attempt to understand Jesus of Nazareth in the light of Christian faith? What questions should be faced and what material should be employed, if one is to expound coherently basic beliefs about Jesus' personal identity and redemptive functions? How can one hope to communicate successfully in this field? What should be the starting-point and centre for the whole process of interpreting Jesus as Son of God and Saviour of the world? In short, what are the requirements for an adequate Christology?

There is obviously the danger here of requiring so much that no Christological product could ever appear satisfactory. A similar set of unreasonable expectations were evident in 1978, after the death of Pope Paul VI. In describing their ideal Bishop of Rome, some commentators listed so many qualities that one wondered how any mere mortal could ever be expected to supply all those requirements. Without setting the standards impossibly high, what are we entitled to look for in current Christian interpretations of Jesus?

1. The Human Condition
Christian beliefs about Jesus focus on someone who was located in a *particular* history and culture. That history

1

and these beliefs are to be correlated with *general* human experiences, questions, sufferings and hopes. If Christian faith in Jesus promises to make sense of life and offer a new understanding of basic human experiences, we need to clarify those experiences, and explore the link between faith in Jesus of Nazareth and the mystery of the human condition.

In the second volume of his *Systematic Theology, Existence and the Christ* (Chicago, 1957), Paul Tillich (1886–1965) used his method of correlation to link an analysis of existential alienation and self-destructiveness with the new being offered by Jesus as the Christ. Even if they do not take up Tillich's term 'method of correlation', when interpreting who Jesus Christ was/is in himself (Christology) and what he has done to save human beings and their world (soteriology), most scholars nowadays systematically correlate their beliefs in Christ with an in-depth examination of the human condition. They expound beliefs about Jesus' personal identity and redemptive functions in association with the ultimate questions and experiences that men and women must face. Thus Walter Kasper (b. 1933) correlates faith in Jesus Christ with the human experience of evil and the quest for freedom and meaning. In a less strictly philosophical way, Jon Sobrino (b. 1938) links the Gospel message about Christ with the situation of Latin Americans who suffer oppression and struggle for justice.

This method of correlation works as an 'apologetic' (in the positive sense of that word), and does so in three distinguishable, if not totally separable, ways: it attempts to show that Jesus Christ is possible, credible and relevant. Among recent writers, no one has surpassed Karl Rahner (1904–84) in illustrating how the incarnation of the divine Logos can be correlated with the ultimate possibilities of human existence. Granted that the incarnation is a free act of divine self-communication, the incarnation is also the absolute culmination of humanity's openness to the infinite God.[1] For more than twenty years Wolfhart Pannenberg (b. 1928) has been concerned to show that Christian beliefs in Jesus credibly meet the demands of scientific reason and truth. Thirdly, in different ways Edward Schillebeeckx and Jon Sobrino present Christ as relevant to the sufferings and needs of human beings.

By showing that in the light of the human condition beliefs about Jesus are intelligible, credible and relevant, the method of correlation necessarily links Christology and soteriology — a point that may put some Christian nerves on red alert. Does this method mean a return to Friedrich Schleiermacher (1768–1834), who made the experience of redemption the basis for Christological — and, indeed, all theological — reflection? In *The Christian Faith* he declared that 'everything is related to the redemption accomplished by Jesus of Nazareth'.[2] More recently, Rudolf Bultmann (1884–1976), Paul Tillich and James Mackey (b. 1934) have pushed the soteriological interest to an extreme. But the way the method of correlation works for Kasper, Rahner and others (including, I hope, myself) entails holding beliefs about Christ's saving function 'for us (*pro nobis*)' in creative tension with beliefs about his personal identity 'in himself (*in se*)'; it does not necessarily mean onesidedly privileging soteriology at the expense of Christology.

Here we should note that any 'apologetic' correlation between some kind of (philosophical and cultural) analysis of the human condition and Christian beliefs about Jesus of Nazareth forms no perfect fit. An analysis of our basic experiences will raise questions about the nature and destiny of human beings in general. But, among other things, the particular story of Jesus includes such shocking surprises as salvation coming through his disgraceful death by crucifixion. In Christology, as elsewhere, we need to remain open to the fact that philosophical questions and findings may be challenged, clarified and changed when they meet the theological answers coming from the full history of Jesus Christ.

3

Before leaving my first requirement for any adequate Christology, let me add two further points. (a) To begin with, the experience and interpretation of the mystery of *evil* will shape deeply any version of the human condition and hence any systematic account of Jesus' identity and saving functions. The triple typology of *death*, *absurdity* and *hatred* offers a workable classification. Whether we witness a fatal accident, watch old age consume a dear friend, see some cherished project collapse before our eyes, or confront death in one of its other innumerable forms, we know that we exist under its ever-present shadow and are constantly threatened with disintegration. Evil often wears the mask of absurdity, falsity and empty meaninglessness. At times, the burden of irrationality and lies may prove even worse than death itself. Then evil also confronts us in the shape of hatred and cold indifference.

In their flight from evil, human beings search for life, meaning and the affirmation of love. In seeking life, meaning and love, men and women are ultimately, I believe, looking for a God whose life is more powerful than any death, whose infinite truth gives final meaning to everything and whose love knows no limits. In Trinitarian terms, this is a quest for the Father, who is the deepest source of all life; the Son, who is Wisdom and the Word of Truth; and the Holy Spirit, who personifies the Love within God that is also communicated to the world.

Seen as a flight from death, absurdity and hatred, and a search for life, meaning and love, the human condition leads us to reflect on the God, who is the source and goal of our existence. Thus (b) the interpretation of our human condition also entails the challenge of thinking and speaking about God. Of course, the history of Jesus will clarify and modify our notions about God. Nevertheless, we do not approach the task of exploring his being truly divine as if we knew nothing about God until we came to Jesus. The story of the Old Testament and the truth to be found in other religions (imperfect and all as they may be) witness to the many ways God can be appreciated before and beyond Christian faith. Other religions have much to say also on the human condition and the evil that threatens it.

In short, to expound basic beliefs about Jesus as Son of God and Saviour of the world, we need to have done some prior work in clarifying the general human condition, the menace of evil and the nature of that God before whom we live and to whom we go.

2. The History of Jesus

After sketching some issues for philosophical reason to examine and clarify, the second requirement concerns the effort to expound and validate Christological faith in its historical origins and development. What can we recover about Jesus' life, death and resurrection? What do we learn from that whole history of interpretation, which began with the earliest Christians and led through the first church councils, down to modern times? Where the method of correlation studies first those human questions, experiences and hopes that illustrate the universal relevance of Christ today, historical research focuses on the past, firstly on the individual Jesus of Nazareth, who exercised a brief ministry before being executed by crucifixion around AD 30.

As a historical religion, Christianity has always recalled and lived by what God revealed and did in the events that make up the total story of Jesus of Nazareth. Nevertheless, from the end of the eighteenth century Christology itself began to be deeply affected by the new discipline of scientific history, and sometimes even destabilised by the rise of critical methods in biblical research. Debates about the earthly Jesus have continued to occupy centre stage. Did he anticipate his violent death and interpret it as redemptively significant for the world? Did the earthly Jesus use 'Son of man' as a self-designation? If so, in what sense(s)? What was his consciousness of his personal identity? Or do the Synoptic Gospels fail to provide any real access whatsoever to his inner life and intentions? Scientific history and exegesis remain prominent dialogue partners of Christology right into the 1980s.

Two related but distinct questions need to be faced here by any Christology. (a) How far can historical scholarship take us in retrieving and reconstructing the ministry, message and fate of the earthly Jesus? (b) To what extent do any conclusions about the historical origins of Christianity feed into and support present faith in the risen Lord? What religious and theological importance do such historical conclusions enjoy?

As regards (a), a broad and growing centre of scholarship has validated a good deal about the activity, claims and impact of Jesus. Joseph Fitzmyer's little classic, *A Christological Catechism. New Testament Answers* (Ramsey, NJ, 1982) , summarises some major items about the history of Jesus that scientific exegesis can properly verify.

However, even after we may have reached satisfactory solutions to historical questions about the earthly Jesus and the origins of Christianity, we are still left with question (b), the role of such historical research for the present formation, interpretation and maintenance of faith in Jesus as Son of God and Saviour of the world. In the late 1970s, *The Myth of God Incarnate* (ed. J. Hick, London, 1977) left many of its readers nervily aware that, in the popular sense of 'myth', the title implied a negative answer to Christian belief in Jesus Christ as divine. But such a reaction missed a key mistake made by some contributors to the book. They seemed to suppose that mere historical inquiry could in principle determine whether or not Jesus of Nazareth was the divine Son of God. Apparently they expected that by providing direct evidence from the New Testament and other documents from past history, such research could simply decide the issue. This was to ask far too much from historical evidence and to forget, among other things, the function of community witness and present experience in affirming the incarnation, the atonement, the resurrection of Jesus and other Christological mysteries.

As I indicated above, systematic reflection on Jesus should also take up conciliar pronouncements about his person and natures: in fact the whole story of the Christian community's traditional faith in and teaching about his personal identity, being and functions. Whether we devote our attention to the New Testament (especially the Gospels) or study the developments of Christological faith and doctrine in the post-apostolic Church, we are making an *historical* approach to Christology. In both cases we are dealing with a remembered and interpreted past.

Certainly in their function and normative value the apostolic and sub-apostolic Church's record and interpretation of Jesus transcend even the most solemn later Church pronouncements about his personal identity and natures. Nevertheless, both Jesus and later teaching about him are known to us through material left by the historical past. In both cases we are in the business of retrieving, understanding and interpreting *particular events*, such as the Last Supper, the Crucifixion and the Council of Chalcedon on the strength of the evidence that they have left behind about their existence and nature. In this historical sense the New Testament and Church tradition resemble each other in their contribution to Christology.

3. History and Philosophy

In outlining some elements in section 2 of this chapter, the historical approach to Christology, I am not suggesting it as an alternative to section 1, the more philosophical method of correlation. We are not dealing with two separate authorities: (2) some specific historical events concerning Jesus (as witnessed to and recorded by the first Christians and then interpreted in post-apostolic Christianity), and (1) the common experience of the human condition (which is constantly threatened with evil but can always lead us to God), a condition that can be interpreted and clarified philosophically. No Christology should oppose an 'historical authority' (the once-and-for-all encounter with God in Jesus of Nazareth) to a 'philosophical authority' (the universally relevant concerns that faith in Christ promises to satisfy today). Instead, what historical research and understanding have to say about the earthly Jesus and the origins of Christianity proves ultimately significant when confronted with our deepest questions, needs and hopes about human life and destiny as such. In the particular story we find the universal answer: Jesus is the Christ.

A further motive for not separating the two approaches comes from the very nature of historical understanding itself. Whenever we seek to investigate and recapture the past, at least implicitly we are always engaged in an exercise of self-understanding and self-interpretation. We use history to evaluate and express the life we have now, the experiences we face at present. It is simply not possible to separate considerations about what happened then and what it all meant then from reflections on what happens now and what it all means now. This can be promptly applied to Christology. The process of establishing things about Jesus' history (and the historical tradition of Christological interpretation) brings investigators to discover things in their own history. They can hardly take up, for example, historical issues about Jesus' death and its atoning value without committing themselves on that mysterious and moving question: What can it mean to say that a crucifixion that took place two thousand years ago representatively expiated our sins and reconciled us with God, with ourselves and with one another?

Here we might take advantage of the parallel to be found in the Old Testament Scriptures. God's people were not satisfied to include only the historical and prophetic books, which dealt largely, albeit not exclusively, with particular events in their story. Undoubtedly, they understood and interpreted themselves primarily in the light of what they believed God to have done in various historical episodes. But they supplemented that knowledge of God and self through the wisdom reflections on the meaning of such common human experiences as material success and failure, family relations, sexual activity and death. Without pressing matters too far, we might accept this parallel: the Old Testament historical/prophetic record stands to the wisdom philosophers' teaching on the human condition as an historical approach to Jesus stands to philosophical reflection on our common human condition. An adequate Christology needs the philosophical *and* the historical components.

4. Eschatology

In both cases the correlation between history and philosophy remains partial and provisional. In the Old Testament story of God's people, the historical and 'philosophical' considerations were eventually modified by the rise of apocalyptic thought. The sign of a general resurrection and judgement to come stood over all that the Israelites grew to know about themselves and their God, either through specific events of history or through the reflections of the wisdom philosophers. Analogously, the future end of all things looms over what the particular history of Jesus and general experience of human beings communicate to us. Jesus preached a divine rule to be consummated in the future, and then his resurrection anticipated the eschaton. His history and what we know of it remain incomplete until that end comes (1 Corinthians 15:20–8). Similarly, any reflections on the deepest human experiences, especially our common human experiences of life, meaning and love, yield only partial glimpses of the reality to be found fully only in the future.

In short, healthy Christology must be not only philosophical and historical, but also eschatological in its approach. Examining at depth our common human condition, we can aim now at recovering and interpreting the historical past of Jesus inasmuch as that past promises us a new and glorious future. In its own way, Christology entails remembering the death of the risen Lord until he comes (1 Corinthians 11:26).

This chapter has outlined the place of philosophical, historical and eschatological elements in the construction of a workable Christology. The next chapter completes my list of things required from any Christology that would systematically interpret Jesus today.

2
CENTRING
AND
COMMUNICATING

Two years ago a prominent Protestant theologian and leader complained to me about the way students for the ministry in his community become impoverished as communicators of Christ: 'We take away their imagination and fill them with concepts.' He could have been talking about what happens practically everywhere in the teaching and writing of theology and, specifically, in the communication of Christology. We take away people's living images of Christ and fill them with abstract concepts about him.

In this chapter I want to list and explore some further requirements for an adequate Christology. In particular, what approaches will enable us to elucidate and communicate more successfully our common beliefs about Jesus Christ as Son of God and Saviour of the world? But before presenting some suggestions for a more communicative style of Christology, I need to reflect briefly on its starting-point and centre.

1. The Centre of Christology

About the starting-point and centre of Christology, differences have hardened into permanent positions. A number of theologians, such as Jean Galot and John Macquarrie, still find a central focus in the incarnation. Others, such as Hans Küng, James Mackey, Edward

Schillebeeckx and Jon Sobrino, take the ministry of Jesus to be the heart of the matter. Walter Kasper, Wolfhart Pannenberg and others (myself included) defend a paschal Christology for which the events of Good Friday and Easter Sunday are decisive.

The liturgy clearly supports starting with the paschal mystery and centring Christological thinking there. From the outset Christians knew themselves to be baptised into the death, burial and resurrection of Jesus (Romans 6:3–5). Their celebration of the Eucharist meant proclaiming the death of our Lord until he comes again (1 Corinthians 11:26). Today at a Roman Catholic Mass in the Latin rite the acclamations after the consecration embody the same faith: 'Lord, by your cross and resurrection you have set us free.' The faithful do not say, 'Incarnating you destroyed our death, preaching you restored our life.' Of course, the birth and ministry of Jesus are vitally important and should never be neglected. But a liturgically based Christology will take shape around the crucifixion and resurrection of Jesus and the basic Christian faith that proclaims: 'Dying you destroyed our death, rising you restored our life.' From that midpoint it can look backwards (through his life, incarnation and the history of the people right back to creation itself), and forwards (through the coming of the Holy Spirit and the story of the Church on to the future consummation of all things).

The Church's worship provides the decisive argument for centring Christology on the resurrection of the crucified Jesus. It also offers illuminating and liberating communication. Before indicating some liturgical, experiential and scriptural possibilities for a more imaginative and communicative Christology, let me state certain convictions about communication and symbolism.

2. Communication and Symbolism

(a) *Communication* is a matter not only of transmitting

information, but also of interpreting experience and thus sharing (and constructing) meaning together, often with a view to common action. Let me offer two examples that can serve to illustrate this description of communication.

A striking example of such real communication comes from Latin America since the 1950s. The Catholic Church and some of the Protestant churches have promoted infrastructures of organisation and communication among the *campesinos* (rural peasants) and, to some extent, among the urban lower classes. A major aim of all this has been to enable such impoverished groups not only to transmit information among themselves, but also to interpret the structural causes of the injustices that they suffer and so to change that situation through shared ideals and common action.

To implement such communication, Christian groups and individuals have established hundreds of local radio stations to be 'the voice of the voiceless' and to initiate radio school systems. Animators have been trained in centres for group communication. Simple printing methods have been developed to produce and distribute local documentation and other materials. In these and other organised ways, communications have been intensified through exchanging information and meaning, which will make shared action possible and effective.

As much as any book ever written, John's Gospel offers an exquisite example of real communication. In all those encounters between Jesus and various individuals, information is certainly transmitted. For instance, he discloses his messianic identity to the Samaritan woman (4:26) and tells another that he is the Son of man (9:35–7). Nevertheless, in the Johannine version of things, communication goes beyond the mere exchange of information to interpret experience and fashion new meaning. For the woman at Jacob's well, Jesus interprets the meaning of such things as a Jew speaking with a Samaritan and a human life scarred by successive marital breakdowns (4:7–26). With Martha and Mary, Jesus reflects on what the death of their brother might ultimately mean (11:1–44).

In these and other encounters, Jesus neither dominatingly imposes his chosen interpretation nor manipulates the other into agreeing with him. Certainly his initiative and divine authority are decisive. But all the same the other must become a free partner in the dialogue and in the shared search for meaning. Chapter 9 yields a striking instance of such a free and, indeed, courageous quest for meaning. After curing the blind man, Jesus leaves the scene. In John's Gospel there is no other section in which he is so long off-stage (9:7b–34). The man who now sees begins to reflect, speak and act with simple vigour. He moves from meaning to meaning, from truth to truth. He first recognises 'the man called Jesus' (9:11) as 'a prophet' (9:17) and 'from God' (9:33). Finally, he understands the ultimate meaning of what has happened and comes to full faith: 'Lord, I believe' (9:38).

What leads the man born blind to that point is his willingness to trust experience and reflect on it in discovering the meaning of his being healed and the identity of the healer. Like many Latin American *campesinos*, he must suffer for his desire to seek and construct meaning. The religious authorities badger the man born blind, and in the name of God's sacred laws try to force him to agree that Jesus is a sinner. After all, the healing work has taken place on the sabbath. But the man born blind stands his ground and insists on the meaning of what he has experienced: 'Whether he is a sinner, I do not know; one thing I know, that though I was blind, now I see.' Further reflection on this experience makes him realise the truly startling nature of what has happened: 'Never since the world began has it been heard that anyone opened the eyes of a man born blind. If this man were not from God, he could do nothing' (9:25, 32–3). When Jesus returns, the communication reaches its climax, as the man born blind grasps the full meaning of his experience and in faith acknowledges Jesus as 'Lord' (9:38).

In these Johannine paradigmatic cases, communication ends with some action. The Samaritan woman goes into the city to invite people to share her experience of Jesus (4:28–30). The man born blind is expelled from the synagogue (9:34). Their communication with Jesus closes when Martha and Mary bring him home to a supper, during which Mary anoints his feet (12:1–8).

John's Gospel finishes with a classic case: the communication between Jesus and Peter (21:1–19). The apostle painfully reconstructs the meaning of his existence as he learns to interpret and integrate his failure and brokenness. Thus he will be able to act by caring for the Master's flock and facing the death by which he is to glorify God. From beginning to end, John's Gospel exemplifies the nature of such real interpersonal communication.

(b) A word about *symbolism*. The primary language of communication is the symbolic: perceptible images that effectively re-present some reality and invite us to participate in it. We did not need to wait for the arrival of television and the image-industries to appreciate the need of symbols for any kind of engaging and transforming communication. John tells symbolic stories about Jesus. The Hebrew Scriptures are full of symbolic events and persons. Let me tell you about one symbolic Saturday morning that succeeded in finally communicating to me a truth about the Church.

Last October I was blessed by the chance of celebrating a wedding in St Peter's basilica in Rome. The bride was Japanese, the bridegroom Australian. After the wedding ceremony and the Eucharist, we walked out of the huge church into the square to have some photographs taken on the steps, under the obelisk and by the fountains. The sun came out, warming thousands of visitors, who were gazing at the majesty of St Peter's, ambling across the cobblestones or moving slowly back

15

to their buses. The newly married couple, especially the bride, changed all that in a moment.

For an hour the radiantly beautiful girl in her long, classical wedding-dress became the centre of St Peter's Square. That Saturday morning she put a smile on thousands of faces. A crowd of Italian teenagers ran up to wish her long life and happiness. A line of Korean tourists greeted her with enthusiasm. Europeans, Africans and Americans swept towards her with their congratulations. With charming courtesy many asked if they might be allowed to photograph the young couple. The whole world seemed to be there rejoicing in their marriage.

What drew that reaction from those thousands of people? The special beauty of the bride in her exquisite white gown obviously touched their hearts. Then the sight of two young persons committing themselves to each other for a lifetime always proves a powerful sign of hope in a world where the future can look precarious and lasting fidelity in short supply. In this case, everyone could see that it was an interracial marriage, between a Japanese and someone of European origin. The decision of the couple to pledge themselves across cultural and national divisions signalled a courageous love that would deal with any difficulty and pay any price. Finally, the unexpected grace of it all must have spoken to many pilgrims and tourists. Who had promised them that they would meet and greet a lovely bride that sunny morning in St Peter's Square?

Thinking later about the whole experience, I found it throwing fresh light on the New Testament's language about all of us in the Church being the bride of Christ. Our community is the 'glorious' spouse of the risen Lord (Ephesians 5:27) and is moving towards the future, heavenly Jerusalem to 'come down out of heaven made ready like a bride adorned for her husband' (Revelation 21:2; see 21:9).

Here and now the Church is called to attract the

16

whole world by her bridal beauty. What is lovely and radiant always evokes joy in others. The Church's radiant devotion to Christ should do just that: draw together the peoples of the earth and put smiles on their faces. Wherever her faithful commitment to the Lord shines out, it will powerfully express hope to a world in which fear, greed and infidelity threaten us all with destruction.

St Paul knew that Christ had put an end to the old barriers that had separated people for so long: 'There is no such thing as Jew and Greek, slave and freeman, male and female; for you are all one person in Christ Jesus' (Galatians 3:28). Those who rejoiced at the young couple in St Peter's Square last October could have said something like that: 'In Christ there is no such thing as Japanese or Australian, for they are made one through their courageous love.' The marriage of my two friends symbolised the new unity of the Christian community, which overcomes deadly divisions through the fresh life of the resurrection.

From the beginning of Christianity, the whole Church has been pictured as Christ's bride. But such images can become routine phrases that lose their power. The unexpected grace of a lovely Japanese girl in St Peter's Square last October put life back into that image for me. She symbolised for me and others what the Church is and is invited to be: a radiant bride who joyfully draws all nations to her risen Lord.

3. Communicative Christology

Where should a truly communicative and symbolic Christology turn and what should it look like? Ultimately, I believe, it should centre around Christ's meaningful presence. His presence can be symbolised and communicated liturgically, experientially and scripturally. Of course, community worship, human experience and the inspired Scriptures cannot be sharply separated. But we should distinguish these three means for communicating symbolically the meaningful presence of Christ.

(a) According to the Synoptic Gospels, Jesus aimed to mediate to his audience the merciful presence of his Father. He never said, 'I am the kingdom.' It was only indirectly that Jesus communicated himself, through what was implied in his words, deeds and personal presence. In a similar way, the Church has to share Christ with the world, communicating herself only indirectly through her worship, preaching and whole activity.

In particular, through her liturgy the Church community enacts and mediates symbolically Christ's presence. Unlike some theological language, which functions to keep people from experiencing his presence, liturgical words and actions aim to evoke, communicate and interpret the experience of that presence. In Christian worship, people celebrate in various ways their encounter with the risen Christ. In that setting he is experienced as the present (1 Corinthians 12:3) and coming Lord (1 Corinthians 16:22).

Beyond question it is difficult to communicate one's human experience. Especially when we are dealing with our religious experience of Jesus Christ, we will always be left with something indescribable and ineffable, which will evade adequate communication. Nevertheless, when the living community celebrates in worship its experience of the risen Lord, it can use a whole range of collective symbols to express that experience and define its meaning. Christology cannot afford to ignore these liturgical symbols. Otherwise it may never succeed in communicating and interpreting Christ's meaningful presence.

(b) Style and beauty characterise or should characterise liturgy. Afghanistan, Auschwitz, El Salvador, Hiroshima and many other places, however, recall and symbolise another contemporary presence of Christ: in the painful ugliness of *suffering*. Admittedly, his presence is not confined to the victims of our world. Yet they remain privileged signs and symbols of the Son of man who identifies himself in a special way with the losers and the needy (Matthew 25:31 ff). Any contemporary Christology would miss much if it systematically ignored the major forms of human experience and, specifically, the presence of Christ mediated through the world's victims.

Christology would do well also to look to a somewhat similar presence of Christ — in the *folly* of saints and prophets. Figures such as Francis of Assisi, John Wesley, Dietrich Bonhoeffer and Mother Teresa of Calcutta offer ways for experiencing something of the Son of God and Saviour of the world. Their lives have symbolised the folly of the cross, which is 'the power of God' (1 Corinthians 1:18) and represented him who 'was crucified in weakness, but lives by the power of God' (2 Corinthians 13:4). The holy madness of such persons forms a living commentary on the crucified and risen Son of man.

(c) Finally, the symbols and symbolic narratives of the *Scriptures* express and define the meaning of Christ and ourselves by bringing us into his communicative presence.

To use again the biblical book already introduced above, John repeatedly pictures a communicative presence in action. The encounters that occur in that Gospel show Christ inviting people to perceive and define their situation by integrating him into their construction of meaning. Nicodemus (3:1–21), the Samaritan woman (4:7–30), the official whose son is ill (4:46–54), Mary Magdalene (20:1–2, 11–18) and the other individuals who meet Jesus are called to make sense of their situation by letting him be *the* Interpreter of their human experiences. He proves himself to be the Light of the World (8:12) by involving them in his presence and interpreting their religious doubt (for Nicodemus), marital breakdown (for the Samaritan woman), a sickness in the family (for the official) and the tragic death of a beloved friend and teacher (for Mary Magdalene).

One might adapt John's prologue to take 'the Word' as 'the Meaning' and say: 'The Meaning became flesh and dwelt among us, full of communication and interpretation. Through experiencing his meaningful presence, we came to know the Father and our own identity.'

Nowadays, most Christologies pull in a great deal of biblical material. In particular, they draw extensively on the New Testament in discussing questions about Jesus himself and the rise of Christian beliefs in him. Nevertheless, I wonder whether they attend adequately to the biblical images and symbolic narratives as such. To the extent that they fail to do so, they will not succeed in evoking and interpreting Jesus' communicative and meaningful presence.

To sum up this chapter. Communication is essential to Christology. Especially in the world of mass communication, any Christology that fails to communicate must be judged sadly deficient. In positive terms, a communicative Christology will follow and live off the images and symbols that fill the Church's liturgy, human experience (and, in particular, the ugly experience of suffering) and the inspired Scriptures. Such a Christology will share meaning, and as in John's Gospel find communication happening in and through the person who is the Interpreter of all our experiences.

In these two opening chapters I have laid out what appear to be the requirements for an adequate Christology in any part of the world. What of local Christologies? What are the challenges and chances for a Christology that looks to the local scene for its inspiration? I turn next to examine the possibilities for such a local Christology in one nation, Australia.

3
CHRISTOLOGY DOWN UNDER

For those of Christian faith, any 'local' theology may appear neither desirable nor possible. So, let me explain.

From its origins, Christianity has stressed times, dates and history. Jesus was born during the reign of Caesar Augustus (Luke 2:1), died by crucifixion while Pontius Pilate was governor of Judaea (AD 26–36), and rose again 'on the third day'. Sunday became the first day of the week for Christians, while their Easter celebrations generally coincided with the date of the Jewish Passover festival. It is perfectly clear that time and history enter deeply into the making and life of Christianity.

But what of space and specific places? Are they so marginal to Christian faith as to render suspect any attempt to fabricate a 'local' theology? Jesus' words to the Samaritan woman seem to redefine our relationship to God in such a way as to dismiss the significance of local settings: 'Woman, believe me, the hour is coming when neither on this mountain nor in Jerusalem will you worship the Father' (John 4:21). The new style of worship 'in spirit and truth' looks as if it minimises the importance of particular places (John 4:23–4).

All the same, Christianity has not robbed specific places of their relevance. When Jesus died at 'the ninth hour' (Mark 15:33 f, 37), he died on a cross at 'the place of the skull' (Mark 15:22, 24). Golgotha stood only a short distance from the rock-tomb where the mystery of the resurrection would take place. The primitive Christian communities ranged from the mother church in the holy city of Jerusalem through the Pauline churches of Asia Minor and Greece to Rome, the scene of martyrdom for Peter and Paul. The letters to the seven churches, the dirge over Babylon, the vision of the New Jerusalem and much else besides in the Book of Revelation clearly illustrate how places and spatial symbols continue to hold their own to the very end of the Bible.

The continuing role of cities and other places for Christian faith stands against anyone who would summarily dismiss a consciously local theology as undesirable. Yet is it feasible? One way of answering this question is to sketch — at least in part — some elements for a local theology, an Australian-style Christology.

1. Some Difficulties

After his two days among them, many Samaritans told the woman who first brought Jesus to their notice: 'It is no longer because of your words that we believe, for we have heard for ourselves, and we know that this is indeed the Saviour of the world' (John 4:42). After two centuries of European settlement, can Australian theologians say to those who taught them: 'It is no longer because of your courses and books that we understand and interpret Jesus, for we have reflected on our experience of him, interpreted his meaningful presence in Australia and can now communicate in our own way the Saviour of the world'?

In theology, as much as in other areas, Australian life and thought has often looked like a provincial and dependent culture. Long after it ceased to be a political colony, Australia has remained a cultural colony. Books, ideas and lecturers pour in from overseas. This theological cargo cult can make Australians good at reporting what Moltmann, Pannenberg, Rahner and Sobrino have to say about the Son of God and Saviour of the world. But truly local answers to the question,

22

'Who do you say that I am?' are still in short supply. Can we contribute as well as consume Christology?

Australia's place on the globe makes things harder. In our Southern Hemisphere Easter comes at the wrong time of year: in autumn. Nevertheless, the Divine Office for Lent and Eastertide, officially approved for use not only in the British Isles but also in Australia and New Zealand, includes the following sixth-century hymn for Morning Prayer:

Jesus, the sun of ransomed earth,
Shed in our inmost souls thy light,
As in spring days a fairer birth
Heralds, each morn, the doom of night.

The day is come, the accepted day,
When grace, like nature, flowers anew;
Trained by thy hand the surer way
Rejoice we in our spring-time too.

In 'The Great Hunger', a poem about rural poverty and religion, Patrick Kavanagh reaches for the language of spring to depict the faith of Irish farmers in the resurrection:

Yet sometimes when the sun comes through a gap
These men know God the Father in a tree:
The Holy Spirit is the rising sap,
And Christ will be the green leaves that will come
At Easter from the sealed and guarded tomb.

It is hardly surprising that in the last century some Australian Christians proposed changing the date of Easter to September and October, even if that meant being out of step with the vast majority of Christians, in the Northern Hemisphere. They wanted to reap the traditional benefits of spring in celebrating the Lord's resurrection.

In Australia the timing seems just as wrong with the

second great event of the Christian year, Christmas. How can one sing 'See, amid the winter's snow' and remember 'the first Noel' on 'a cold winter's night that was so deep', when the temperature outside stands at thirty degrees Celsius and there is a smell of bushfires in the air? The blazing heat of an Australian December makes Christina Rossetti's Christmas carol locally incongruous:

> In the bleak midwinter,
> frosty wind made moan,
> earth stood hard as iron,
> water like a stone;
> snow had fallen, snow on snow,
> snow on snow,
> in the bleak midwinter
> long ago.

As well as being culturally and liturgically disadvantaged, Australians may wonder where to find *local* tragic heroes who can help us gain insight into the story of Jesus' victory coming through apparent defeat and public failure. An expeditionary tradition took young Australian soldiers right out of the country to fight and die thousands of miles away during the Boer War, World War I, World War II, the Korean War and the Vietnam War. Recent Australian films settle for this image of the champion who does not die at home but overseas, such as Breaker Morant in South Africa and Archy on the battlefield of Gallipoli. Heroes, it seems, do not shed their blood on our own soil. They go overseas to die.

When the Australian novelist Thomas Keneally wrote about a flawed but noble 'redeemer', he found him in Europe during World War II. A British plane piloted by an Australian came down on the edge of Oskar Schindler's camp in Cracow, but otherwise Australia never touched the story of the hero of *Schindler's Ark*, a promiscuous German industrialist who saved hundreds of Jews and even managed to rescue some from Auschwitz.

2. Some Advantages

It is all too easy to rattle on, listing the difficulties against constructing a genuinely Australian Christology. So, often, local theologians have been content to reiterate ideas from overseas. Our nation itself comes across to many as a land of material bounty and spiritual waste. But, instead of grumbling about these and other problems, I want to spend time on some genuine advantages or at least possibilities for those who want to develop Christology here. There are things and experiences that offer an Australian access to the good news about Jesus and systematic reflection on his person and redemptive work.

(a) Last year in Israel I noticed how Australia had left its mark physically on places connected with Jesus. The Church of the Holy Sepulchre contains two bronze doors 'donated by the people of Australia'. Up north in Nazareth, mosaics given by Christians from many countries cover the walls of the modern Basilica of the Annunciation. Alongside works from Japan, Poland and the United States, there is a large and lovely Australian mosaic of Mary and the Child Jesus.

All over the Holy Land, Australian gum-trees offer shade and sweeten the air. They flank the road that leads across the Plain of Esdraelon towards Nazareth. They give shelter on the Mount of Beatitudes, and fill the ground between the ruins of Capernaum and the Sea of Galilee. At a bend in the Jordan where many pilgrims enter the waters to renew their baptismal vows, gum-trees tower over the river and fill the air with the scent of eucalyptus. On the road going down from Jerusalem to Jericho, an ancient stone enclosure, called The Good Samaritan Inn, tops a rise and looks across folding valleys where over the centuries bandits often concealed themselves. Right outside the inn a chunky gum-tree offers the traveller a little relief from the heat and the flies.

In World War I Australian Light Horsemen fought near Jericho. In World War II Australian soldiers came to Jerusalem on leave or passed through Palestine en route to military operations in Lebanon.

Admittedly, all these links through trees, church art and military history are recent. But they draw attention to a certain similarity (not identity) in climate and terrain. Like the land of Jesus, Australia has its fertile plains, but is often a hot, dry country, where flies abound , water is scarce, deserts spread and rivers end in salt lakes. Such similarities in geography and climate can play their role in facilitating an imaginative leap to the history of Jesus. As such, white Australians are a modern phenomenon. They have less than two hundred years of tenure behind them. But the country they took over yields some perspective on the environment in which Jesus lived out his story. The coming of Australian gum-trees to the Holy Land symbolises that affinity.

(b) The geography and recent history of Australia itself yield other perspectives on the story of Jesus. This island-continent is well over three hundred times the size of Israel, but Australia's setting helps us to gain a little insight into the environment into which Jesus was born. Israel lived under the shadow of huge neighbours: Assyria, Babylon, Egypt, Persia and, finally, the Roman Empire. At times, the Jewish people had to put aside other considerations and concentrate on showing loyalty to some protecting power. Unlike Israel, Australia has all her giant neighbours to the north. Nevertheless, their presence has constantly raised the question for Australians: Who can help us to survive the pressure of all these people?

Without demanding an excessive leap of the imagination, one can also note an Australian analogy to that central symbol of Jesus' people: the exodus from suffering and oppression to a land of freedom. The large ethnic communities in Australia act as a constant reminder that so many recently arrived people came to escape from poverty, oppression and danger. The 1976 national census showed Australia to be, in proportional terms, the second largest host country in the world for post-World War II migrants. Twenty per cent of the population was born overseas. Another twenty per cent had one or both parents born overseas. Only modern Israel has a higher proportion of post-World War II migrants.

As in the case of the original Exodus, many modern refugees suffered not only en route to Australia, but also following their arrival. After the Aborigines, migrant workers have been the most socially and economically disadvantaged group in the country.

The Vietnamese boat-people, who in such numbers between 1976 and 1979 literally came through the water to safety, brought the image of an exodus from bondage right up to date. The experience of these refugees gave fresh life to that basic religious symbol for Jesus and his people: the coming away from oppression and passing through the sea to freedom. Australia shares no land boundaries. Like others before them, the Vietnamese had to make their exodus and cross the water to reach this island-continent. Theologians who are responsive to the place of migration right down to very recent events in Australian history could find here a language to present imaginatively both the original coming out of Egypt and Jesus' own passover through death to new life. By continuing to refurbish the image of the exodus, the Australian story offers that help to anyone who sets out to interpret the person of Jesus and the deliverance that he celebrated in Jewish worship, experienced for himself in the paschal mystery and communicates to us now under sacramental signs.

In thinking of post-World War II immigration, we do

well to remember also its impact on Australian life. It has turned Australia into a multiracial and multicultural society. The new peoples, traditions and languages make the nation a kind of 'Galilee of the Gentiles'. Admittedly one should not press the comparison too far. Unlike the Palestine of Jesus' day, Australia has no foreign army of occupation. Nevertheless, the variety in post-World War II Australian society gives us an easier imaginative access to the pluralistic environment in which Jesus lived, worked and died.

Two further advantages should not be forgotten. Since the nineteenth century, unlike many countries, Australia has enjoyed a substantial Jewish presence. Through this people the special saving activity of God comes into view, the activity that culminated in the story of Jesus himself. In a living, actual way, Australian Jews recall in our midst the whole history of grace that Paul summarises:

They are Israelites, and to them belong the sonship, the glory, the covenants, the giving of the law, the worship, and the promises; to them belong the patriarchs, and of their race, according to the flesh, is the Christ.
(Romans 9:4–5)

The apostle here uses the present tense ('belong'), for not only does this race take us back to the special history of salvation recounted and interpreted by the Scriptures, but it also remains here and now unique in God's sight. 'As regards election', Paul writes, 'they are beloved for the sake of their forefathers. For the gifts and call of God are irrevocable' (Romans 11:28–9). An Australian Christology, if it is to be true to Jesus' Jewishness, must take into account his brothers and sisters who live among us and are one major way of bringing his presence to us.

Lastly, the Moslem population has grown significantly in recent years. Currently there must be over 200,000 Moslems living in Australia. This post-World

War II development both encourages and facilitates an approach to Christology that would be more 'ecumenical', in that wider sense of dialogue with those believers who do not share the Christian faith. In particular, Moslems share with us 'the faith of Abraham, the father of us all' (Romans 4:16). They honour the Virgin Mary and acknowledge Jesus as prophet and final judge. Their insistence on the divine unity constantly cautions Christians against interpreting the persons of Christ and the Holy Spirit in such a way as would turn our monotheism into a tritheism. Australian Christology both can and should hear the challenging questions of Islam.

3. Space and Time

Great distances separate very many Australians from their cultural origins in Europe or Asia. They live now on an island-continent surrounded by a huge expanse of water in the Southern Hemisphere. Within Australia itself, big distances keep the major cities far from each other. Vast stretches of intimidating desert-land spread across much of the interior.

It is no wonder that Australians often betray a special sense of space. Novels such as Eleanor Dark's *The Timeless Land* and Mary Aeneas Gunn's *We of the Never-Never* suggest how spatial symbols and notions can come more easily to crowd out the language of time. A feeling of living in an empty, isolated environment may make space a challenge to be overcome or even a curse to be exorcised. Witness Geoffrey Blainey's *The Tyranny of Distance*.

If I am right about Australians often having an unusual sense of space and less sense of time, can this be turned to advantage for Christology? The forward, historical thrust of the Jewish-Christian religion seems to tell against the chance of any local theology and, in particular, a local Christology. In Romans and 1 Corinthians, Paul fashions his Christology in an unmistakably futurist key. Christ has been raised from the dead as 'the first fruits of those who have fallen asleep'. Hence his work will continue dynamically until 'the end comes' (1 Corinthians 15:20, 24). The new life given 'in Christ' entails looking in hope to obtain finally 'the glorious liberty of the children of God' (Romans 8:1, 21). The prayer with which the New Testament ends, 'Come, Lord Jesus' (Revelation 22:20), illustrates how the Christological thinking of the early Christians sweeps on through time in worshipping Jesus Christ, 'the same yesterday and today and for ever' (Hebrews 13:8). How can those who are more spatially oriented put together a genuine Christology?

It could mean that an Australian Christology should draw particularly on the Captivity Epistles. Without suppressing at all 'temporal' ways of depicting Christ's person and saving work (for example, Colossians 3:4), those letters break easily into the language of 'breadth, length, height and depth' (Ephesians 3:18). One might afford to be imaginative in translating into Australian terms the vision of reconciliation between Jews and Gentiles:

... remember that you were at that time separated from Christ, alienated from the commonwealth of Israel ... But now in Christ Jesus you who once were far off have been brought near in the blood of Christ. For he is our peace, who has made us both one, and has broken down the dividing wall of hostility. (Ephesians 2:12–14)

Just as Christ overcame the religious distance between Jews and Gentiles, so too for Australians his work of reconciliation can mean dealing with and healing that spatial fragmentation from which they can suffer.

At the beginning of this chapter I recalled some examples that establish the permanent significance for Christianity of space and local language. Christian theology in general should be responsive to spatial symbols. Likewise, Australian Christology in particular might well design ways of thinking that could be coupled with the spatial mind-set of Colossians, Ephesians and some other parts of the New Testament.

Nature herself provides a prod in this direction. In our Southern Hemisphere the stars of a vast constellation form the Southern Cross, a great sign 'in the heavenly places' of what God 'accomplished in Christ' (Ephesians 1:20). That sign in the night skies invites Australians to 'set their minds on things that are above' (Colossians 3:2). It could also steer towards a Christology that gives special attention to the language and symbols of peace. In Christ's cross we find our peace and reconciliation (Colossians 1:20).

4
THE
RESURRECTION
OF
JESUS

In Chapter 3 I argued that Christology should centre on Jesus' dying *and rising*. Back in Chapter 1 I pointed out the need to validate Christological faith in its historical origins and development. That entails establishing what we can about Jesus' life, death *and resurrection*. In this chapter I plan to put together and run through some problems that could confront a Christology centred around the paschal mystery. It is simply not possible to raise all the issues. Let me select and concentrate on certain challenges in the fields of history, faith and theology.

1. History
When faced with death, Jesus continued to maintain the validity of his message and his certainty of being saved (Mark 14:25). He interpreted his self-giving as a new covenant, which would be beneficial 'for many' (1 Corinthians 12:23–5; Mark 14:22–4). His male disciples fled when he was arrested (Mark 14:27–8, 50; John 16:32), and an outsider took care of his burial (Mark 15:43). Jesus' crucifixion challenged the interpretation of his coming death and certainty about being saved that he had expressed at the last supper. According to the contemporary interpretation of Deuteronomy

21:23 (see the Qumran Temple Roll 64:6–13 and Galatians 3:13), someone crucified for breaking the law was understood to be cursed by God. But then the disciples began proclaiming that God had raised Jesus from the dead (for example, 1 Thessalonians 1:10; Acts 2:32; Romans 10:9). This proclamation was initiated by appearances of the living Jesus (for example, 1 Corinthians 15:5–8) and, secondarily, by the discovery that his tomb was empty (Mark 16:1–8 and parallels).

Apropos of the Easter appearances and the empty tomb, there are many problems. No doubt it will stay that way till the end of time. Here I want to raise and briefly respond to some questions, so as to illustrate what a resurrection-centred Christology might have to tackle today.

(a) The Appearances
In discussing the appearances, it may be as well to start with the ingenious 'swoon theory', which H. E. G. Paulus floated in the last century and which has enjoyed a number of variants in recent decades. Essentially the hypothesis comes to this. Jesus did not die on the cross, but was taken down alive from the cross, revived in the tomb, somehow got out and 'appeared' to his followers. In his novella *The Man Who Died*, D. H. Lawrence has Jesus coming back in this way to his followers and then slipping off to Egypt to enjoy conjugal relations with a priestess of Isis. Other versions of this 'happy ending' have Jesus going away to live with Mary Magdalene, as in *The Holy Blood and the Holy Grail* by Baigent, Leigh and Lincoln. Some Moslems claim that, after escaping from the tomb, Jesus even reached India; at Srinagar in Kashmir tourists can see a shrine that is alleged to be the place where he was finally buried after really dying in old age.

In *The Anastasis* (Shipston-on-Stour, 1982), Duncan Derrett suggests that Jesus 'entered into a self-induced trance' on the cross (p. 45). Those who buried him took him to be dead, but this 'clinical death' was briefly reversed before irreversible brain-death finally occurred. But he had made significant use of his short-lived recovery. For after he revived in the cold tomb and had been helped out (apparently by some people watching at the tomb and the 'young man' of Mark 16:5–7), he was able to commission his disciples. Shortly thereafter, as a result of his sufferings and crucifixion, he underwent final brain-death. He had authorised his disciples to dispose of his corpse by cremation, and they burnt it outside the walls of Jerusalem. The ascension, as recounted by Luke, was a 'euphemism' for that cremation (pp. 83, 90).

Out here in Australia, Barbara Thiering has also advanced the theory that Jesus did not die on the cross. Her account runs as follows. The vinegar (Mark 15:36) that Jesus was given contained some poison that would eventually have killed him. However, he was placed alive in the tomb with the the two criminals crucified with him. One of these two men (whom Thiering identifies as Simon Magus and Judas Iscariot) administered aloes to Jesus which caused him to bring up the poison. His supporters smuggled Jesus out of the tomb. After spending some years with the early Christian community, he then really died. Finally, Thiering adds her own startling twist to the 'swoon theory'. Jesus' crucifixion, burial and escape from the tomb did not take place in Jerusalem but in or around Qumran.[1]

Against these different versions of the 'swoon theory' it must be said that their major 'source', the New Testament itself, contains not a shred of hard evidence in their favour. The Gospels, St Paul and the primitive Christian kerygma (which gets quoted in 1 Corinthians 15:3b–5, the early speeches in Acts and elsewhere in the New Testament) agree that Jesus genuinely died by crucifixion and was buried as a dead man (for instance, 1 Corinthians 15:4; Mark 15:37, 42–7). Other ancient sources corroborate this. The Jewish historian, Flavius Josephus (AD 37–c.100), in his *Antiquities* 18:63–4 reports that Jesus was crucified on the orders of Pilate. It seems that some Christian or Christians revised this passage in Josephus by adding material in praise of Jesus, but at least the information about his execution seems to go back to Josephus himself. In his *Annals* 15:44 (written in AD 112–113), the Roman historian Tacitus explains that the name 'Christians' came from the founder of their sect, Christ, who was executed by the 'procurator' Pontius Pilate during the reign of the Emperor Tiberius. In an obscure passage, the Babylonian Talmud (*Sanhedrin* 43a) writes of Yeshu, who led some Israelites astray by his magic, but was then 'hanged on the eve of Passover'. These extra-biblical, Roman and Jewish sources show little historical knowledge, but they indicate no doubt whatsoever that Jesus genuinely died by execution. Like the passion narratives in the Gospels, these other documents contain not the slightest hint that Jesus was or could have been still alive when the executioners had finished with him.

In the nineteenth century, David Friedrich Strauss (1808–74) cast many doubts on the gospel story, but even so had no truck with the swoon theory. He put his finger on another knockdown difficulty against any hypothesis of a half-dead Jesus reviving in the tomb and then returning to his followers:

It is impossible that a being who had stolen half dead out of the sepulchre, who crept about weak and ill, wanting medical treatment, who required bandaging, strengthening and indulgence . . . could have given the disciples the impression that he was a Conqueror over death and the grave, the Prince of Life, an impression which lay at the bottom of their future ministry. Such a resuscitation . . . could by no possibility have changed their sorrow into enthusiasm, have elevated their reverence into worship.[2]

Add, too, the fact that neither the New Testament nor any other source provides evidence for the post-crucifixion existence and activity of a Jesus who was revived from apparent death. Derrett admits as much when he writes of 'the loud silence of the gospels and epistles' about Jesus' brief life after his revival from clinical death (*Anastasis*, p. 71).

Before dismissing the whole 'swoon theory' as bogus nonsense, we might reflect briefly on the thinking behind it. Besides expressing a refusal to accept that Jesus truly rose from the dead to a new, transformed life, this theory serves to bring out the nature of historical certainties and a persistent desire that goes right back to the time of the apocryphal gospels.

It is always open to anyone to deny facts that professional scholars and the general public agree on and correctly take for granted. An imagination that does not bother to produce hard evidence for bold assertions can then advance sensational claims and propose ingenious counter-stories. One could, for example, make up a story about Julius Caesar not having been assassinated in 44 BC. Someone else was killed in his place; he escaped to the Tiber and took a trireme to Britain, where he cultivated vineyards and helped to prepare the way for the eventual settlement of the Romans. Absolutely speaking, this counter-story cannot be ruled out as impossible. But the lack of evidence in its favour and the convergent proofs for the normally accepted version of Caesar's untimely end make an escape-to-Britain hypothesis so utterly implausible that it is not worth bothering about. Practically every historian and biblical scholar would say the same thing about the 'swoon theory'.

This theory, I suspect, is fed by a tendency that set in fairly early among some Christians, and which a Californian friend of mine summed up as follows: 'When they ran out of things they knew about Jesus, they started making up and writing down things they really didn't know.' Thus the canonical Gospels knew of no witnesses to the very event of Jesus' resurrection itself. The second-century Gospel of Peter 9:35 ff invents such witnesses. There are so many limits and gaps in what we know about Jesus' life, death and resurrection, that it is tempting to conjecture, fabricate and fill in details that the real evidence does not support. In their variant of the 'swoon theory', R. Graves and J. Podro, for example, generously supply information about 'the extreme sultriness of the weather' (which, together with the spikenard ointment smeared on the shroud, helped to keep Jesus alive in the tomb), and about the way he escaped:

The Roman soldiers, hired to stand guard, rolled back the stone at night while their sergeant was asleep and tried to steal the ointment — which was worth several years' army pay and could easily be sold in the brothels of Cacsarea. They found Jesus still alive, and the sergeant, when acquainted with the surprising news, let him go; being subsequently bribed by Bunni [= the name Graves and Podro give to Nicodemus] to say that the disciples had removed the body. (*Jesus in Rome*, London, 1957, pp. 12–13).[3]

All of this suggests a novelist's anxiety to reconstruct a well-rounded story, although one must be grateful that Graves and Podro do not indulge a taste for *cherchez la femme* and arrange for Jesus to rendezvous with Mary Magdalene or a priestess of Isis.

At the end of the day, the 'swoon theory' reduces the origin of Christianity to a banal story about a bungled execution. In place of the mystery of Jesus' true resurrection from the dead, we are told that he had an incredibly lucky revival from apparent death — a revival that his disciples later misrepresented when they claimed that he had been 'raised from the dead, never again to revert to corruption' (Acts 13:34). The 'swoon theory', by granting Jesus only a temporary respite from death after an extraordinary unpleasant brush with crucifixion, makes the New Testament's language about his glorious, new, incorruptible existence (for instance, 1 Corinthians 15:20 ff; Luke 24:26) simply incomprehensible or else a bold lie.

To keep this section on the risen Lord's appearances

down to manageable proportions, let me next glance quickly at some other current counter-explanations. The hypothesis that the disciples somehow hallucinated the risen Jesus' appearances has been tried and found wanting.[4] Ian Wilson, however, has recently returned to this hypothesis, arguing that

. . . it is possible that he [Jesus] prepared his disciples for his resurrection using the technique that modern hypnotists call post-hypnotic suggestion. By this means he would have effectively conditioned them to hallucinate his appearances in response to certain pre-arranged cues (the breaking of bread?), for a predetermined period after his death. (*Jesus the Evidence*, London, 1984, p. 141.)

Wilson supports his theory by gratuitously attributing such powers of hypnosis to Jesus and throwing in an experiment in post-hypnotic suggestion on one volunteer who 'was known to be a good hypnotic subject' (*ibid*. pp. 141 f). How on earth do we know that the disciples were all such good hypnotic subjects? What of Paul, who saw the risen Christ, but had enjoyed no contact with Jesus during the ministry and hence could not have been conditioned to hallucinate an Easter appearance in response to some pre-arranged cues?

Largely on the basis of the Nag Hammadi papyrus codices (3rd to 5th century AD), James Robinson has proposed that the original Christian tradition told of the risen Christ's disembodied appearances in light on a mountain. But the evidence for such luminous appearances comes from later, gnostic sources, which do not provide us with any independent and trustworthy date about the origins of Christianity.[5]

Since writing *Jesus* (London, 1979), Edward Schillebeeckx has modified his view on the Easter experiences of Peter and the other disciples. According to that book, through the real but invisible influence of the risen Lord, the disciples experienced a deep forgiveness and conversion, which they expressed in the model of 'appearances'. But their talk of 'appearances' was only a means for articulating what the invisible Jesus had done for them after his death and resurrection, and did not refer to genuinely historical events (pp. 354–90).

In his *Interim Report on the Books 'Jesus' and 'Christ'* (New York, 1982), Schillebeeckx concedes that when the first Christians spoke of 'appearances', this 'need not be a pure model; it can also imply a historical event' (p. 147, fn. 43; see p. 148, fn. 46). Nevertheless, he continues to play down the role of such appearances — and, for that matter, of the discovery of the empty tomb — in generating Easter faith:

... belief in the Jesus who is risen and lives with God and among us cannot be founded on an empty tomb as such, nor as such on the visual elements which there may have been in 'appearances' of Jesus. (*ibid.* p. 75)

This statement cries out for some qualification. Of course, other factors, such as their belief in God and their association with Jesus during his ministry, fed into the disciples' new faith in Jesus as risen and living. At the same time, visual appearances and, secondarily, the discovery of the empty tomb triggered off that faith. Schillebeeckx's 'cannot be founded' invites an old-fashioned scholastic distinction: 'Easter faith was not *simply* founded on the appearances and the empty tomb?', Yes; 'This faith was *not in any way* founded on those appearances and that discovery?', No.

Another scholar to change his mind recently on the Easter appearances is Rudolf Pesch. Almost an entire issue of the Tübingen *Theologische Quartalschrift* (153 (1973), pp. 201–83) was given over to Pesch's original presentation on the rise of Easter faith and various reactions to his interpretation. In essence, he denied the historicity of the Easter appearances and argued that the disciples simply applied to the case of Jesus an earlier Jewish tradition about the martyrdom and resurrection of godly persons, especially eschatological prophets. But the evidence for such an earlier tradition is quite uncertain. For that and other reasons, in a 1980 lecture that he contributed to the *Festschrift* for F.-X. Durrwell's seventieth birthday, Pesch withdrew his earlier hypothesis and argued as follows. The visions of the risen Jesus were real events in history. When he appeared to the apostolic witnesses, they saw him in heavenly glory — not as an eschatological prophet who had undergone martyrdom and resurrection, but as the Son of man, who with all power 'sits at the right hand of God' and who will come at the end to judge the world.[6]

One should welcome Pesch's new willingness to accept the factuality of the Easter visions. However, his thesis that Jesus appeared precisely as the Son of man seems thoroughly dubious. Mark's three passion predictions (8:31; 9:31; 10:33 f) speak of the Son of man's death and resurrection, but not of his subsequent appearances as such. When Jesus promises 'You will see the Son of man', he is addressing the high priest and his council (and not any apostolic witnesses to the resurrection) and is talking of the *parousia*: 'You will see the Son of man seated at the right hand of God, and coming with the clouds of heaven' (Mark 14:62). In the transfiguration story (Mark 9:2–13) Pesch finds 'the most impressive proof of the fact that the primitive community knew the visions of the Risen One as visions of the Son of man'.[7] But that story ends with Jesus instructing Peter, James and John 'to tell no one what they had seen until the Son of man should have risen from the dead' (Mark 9:9). Jesus does not say, 'until the Son of man rises from the dead *and appears to you*'.

In a later publication I plan to take up Pesch's new thesis in greater detail. Here let me merely note that I find his exegetical arguments quite forced. Furthermore, he simply ignores the early material, which designates as 'Christ' or 'Lord' (and not as 'Son of man'), the risen Jesus who appeared to the apostolic witnesses (for example, 1 Corinthians 9:1; 15:3–8; Acts 2:23 f, 31–3, 36).

Before leaving the Easter appearances I want to draw attention to a decisive difference between those such as Karl Rahner, Hans Küng and Walter Kasper (who maintain clearly that the first disciples had a unique, unrepeatable experience of the risen Lord) and those such as Schillebeeckx, who neglect or play down the *special* nature of that experience. As we have seen, Schillebeeckx takes the Easter experience of the disciples to be above all a matter of forgiveness and conversion, a 'renewal of life and the experience of Jesus' spiritual presence' (*Interim Report*, p. 78). But obviously this 'experience of the new (spiritual) presence of the risen Jesus in the gathered community' (*ibid.* p. 80) can be shared by any of his followers anywhere and at any time. Peter and the other Easter witnesses were only chronologically the first to experience 'Jesus' new saving presence in the midst of his own people on earth' (*ibid.* p. 81). All later Christians can gather together to know the same forgiveness and conversion through the same, new presence of the risen Lord. However, once the special nature of the Easter appearances gets left behind, the apostolic witnesses cease to be normative interpreters of Jesus' life, death and resurrection and authoritative founders of the Christian church. Schillebeeckx himself seems to point in that direction by remarking that it is only 'for the knowledge [but not for any normative interpretation?] of Jesus in whom we believe' that we depend on these witnesses. They 'have no [other] advantage over us than that they were there at the time' (*ibid.* p. 7).

(b) The Empty Tomb.

After sampling some contemporary theories on the appearances of the risen Jesus, we can move to the issue of the empty tomb. Here it does no harm to recall that, despite sensational reports about Christian scholars denying the empty tomb, a large number of critical exegetes and historians defend it. To give some names:

42

Berten, Blank, Blinzler, Brown, von Campenhausen, Delorme, Fitzmyer, Fuller, Grundmann, Jeremias, Kremer, Künneth, Léon-Dufour, Martini, Moule, Murphy-O'Connor, Mussner, Nauck, Pannenberg, Rengstorff, Rückstuhl, Schenke, Schmitt, Schubert, Schweizer, Seidensticker, Strobel, Stuhlmacher, Trilling, Vögtle and Wilckens.[8] In his 'The Historicity of the Empty Tomb of Jesus', W. L. Craig makes a good, contemporary case for the discovery of Jesus' empty grave being an historical event.[9]

Rather than merely report scholarly supporters, I want also to examine briefly several contrary views. To begin with Schillebeeckx. He correctly draws attention to something already recognised in the New Testament itself: the empty tomb can be explained in various ways — for example, as a case of theft (Matthew 27:62–6; 28:11–15; John 20:1–2, 15) — and hence by itself 'is not evidence for a resurrection' (*Interim Report*, p. 86). However, some distinctions are called for when Schillebeeckx states in an unqualified way, 'The historical discovery of the empty tomb [by itself? even taken together with other reasons?] can never be the foundation of the Christian resurrection faith' (*ibid.*). One of the anti-resurrection *graffiti* that turn up every now and then on city walls correctly implies that for many believers the discovery of the empty tomb, along with other factors, plays its role in supporting their faith: 'There will be no Easter this year. They have found the body.' The fact that the body was not found supports resurrection faith — at least in the sense of clearing the way for it. Schillebeeckx disregards all those people for whose Easter faith the empty grave of Jesus has such a role by decreeing that this 'can never be' so.

Since Schillebeeckx resolutely refuses to let the empty tomb affect the making of *faith*, it is not surprising to hear from him that the tomb (whether empty or not) is *theologically* 'irrelevant for us' (*ibid.* pp. 86 f). Who are the 'we' here? Certainly not myself and others who discover much that is theologically relevant in the fact and

43

symbol of Jesus' empty tomb. I will return to this point shortly.

In *Jesus*, Schillebeeckx opted for the reasonable exegetical hypothesis that a liturgical tradition lay behind Mark 16:1–8. According to that view (endorsed by scholars such as J. Delorme, J. Murphy-O'Connor, W. Nauck and L. Schenke), once a year or perhaps more often, Christians went to the grave of Jesus to celebrate together a liturgy. We know that Jews and others built, honoured and visited the tombs of revered persons such as prophets and martyrs. Curiously, however, Schillebeeckx seems to think that such a liturgical hypothesis rules out the emptiness of Jesus' tomb: 'The new problem is whether we have a tradition of an "empty tomb" *or* [italics mine] a tradition of the "holy tomb" ' (*Jesus*, p. 703, fn. 32). Such an alternative simply ignores one major reason for supposing that Mark drew on a liturgical tradition: the words 'He has been raised again; he is not here; see the place where they laid him' (Mark 16:6). It requires no great leap of the imagination to hear these words being spoken at Jesus' tomb by the president of the liturgy. If we agree that such is the origin of these words, then the liturgical tradition of the 'holy tomb' necessarily involves the historical tradition of an 'empty tomb'. It seems to me inconceivable that the president of the liturgy could have said, 'he is not here; see the place where they laid him', if the bones of Jesus were there in the tomb. In *this* case, to choose the hypothesis of cult at the tomb logically means accepting the emptiness of the tomb. Schillebeeckx misses various points of difference when he mentions the 'countless examples in antiquity' of 'pilgrimages to the tomb of a revered "hero" ' (*Interim Report*, p. 86). It was, for example, only in the case of Jesus that the leader of the pilgrimage said, 'He has been raised again; he is not here; see the place where they laid him.'

At Harvard Divinity School, Dieter Georgi developed his particular thesis on Jesus' tomb, a thesis expounded by a colleague (Helmut Koester) on 22 April 1984 during the third part of the British television programme *Jesus, the Evidence.* The Georgi–Koester view goes as follows. (i) Until the mid-sixties Christians worshipped at the tomb of Jesus, which contained his bones. (ii) Around that time the tomb became empty. Jewish opponents may have stolen the remains, or others (Romans?) may have removed them to prevent possible political disturbances. Or the Christians themselves, when they left Jerusalem in AD 66, may have taken Jesus' remains with them. (iii) However it happened that the remains were removed, Christians ceased praying at Jesus' tomb and excused this lack of worship by explaining that the tomb was empty. (iv) Then, 'as the Gospels were written down years later, the story [about Jesus' tomb no longer containing his mortal remains and Christians no longer worshipping there] quickly began to serve a different purpose. It began to be used to suggest the tomb had always been empty.'

As regards (iii), one wonders why after AD 66 the Christians did not excuse themselves by explaining that a ferocious war prevented their going back to Jerusalem, or — even more simply — by producing the remains of Jesus, which, according to Georgi and Koester, they may have taken with them. However, it is even more apropos of (iv) that the Georgi–Koester theory deserves to be challenged. 'Years later' implies a decade or more from AD 66 until the composition of the first Gospel (Mark) and then the other three Gospels. Almost all scholars date the writing of Mark's Gospel to AD 70, or even some years earlier, in the sixties. If Georgi and Koester are serious about 'years later', by dating Mark after AD 75 they would probably find themselves in a minority of two. Furthermore, Georgi and Koester accept that Mark took over a pre-existing story about Jesus' tomb. But in the pre-Markan material, which can be identified in Mark 16:1–8, there is not the slightest trace of an explanation by Christians that they no longer worshipped at Jesus' tomb *because* they or others had taken away his mortal remains. *If* Georgi and Koester are right, we would expect something of that explanation to have come through.

Finally, the source for Mark 16:1–8 seems much older than a story created after AD 66. A number of considerations suggest dating the composition of that tradition (not the same as the even earlier event, which the tradition relates) to the first decade of Christianity. Unlike 1 Corinthians 15:4 or Acts 2:25–8, that pre-Markan tradition does not 'prove' the resurrection from scripture. Unlike 1 Corinthians 15:3b or Luke 24:26, it uses no Christological titles, but simply refers to 'Jesus of Nazareth, who was crucified' (Mark 16:6). Unlike Matthew 28:11–15, it does not indulge in apologetics and polemics. In these three ways the tradition behind Mark 16:1–8 comes across as theologically simple, and hence from the early years of Christianity. The way of dating the women's visit to the tomb, 'on the first day of the week' (Mark 16:2), as opposed to the standard expression for the resurrection, 'on the third day' (or 'after three days'), may also be a sign of the tradition's antiquity. Likewise the passive form of 'has been raised again, *ēgerthē*' (Mark 16:6) can also suggest the earliest way of expressing the resurrection as God (the Father) raising Jesus from the dead (for example, 1 Thessalonians 1:10; Romans 10:9; Galatians 1:1). All in all, it comes across as thoroughly dubious to date to AD 66 or later the tradition used in Mark 16:1–8.

Let me finish this sampling of historical questions by selecting another view, which may be unsatisfactory but does lead us towards some basic theological issues. Apropos of Jesus' corpse, Hans Küng takes the empty tomb to be unlikely and, indeed, unnecessary:

There can be identity of the person even without continuity between the earthly and the 'heavenly', 'spiritual' body . . . The corporality of the resurrection does not require the tomb to be empty. (*On Being a Christian*, London, 1976, p. 366)

Here Küng defends a corporeal resurrection, but dispenses with any *bodily* continuity between the earthly and risen existence of Jesus. The totally new 'spiritual' body comes into existence without any continuity with the former, earthly body, and yet without imperilling the genuinely personal identity of Jesus. In his risen state he is identical with, and no mere substitute for, the person who died on the cross and was buried. Küng seems to locate Jesus' continuity simply at the level of soul or spirit. The new, 'heavenly' body totally replaces the one that ended in the tomb.

In Küng's statement 'can' and 'require' are tell-tale words. As such he speaks at the level of principle: of what God *could* do. In theory the resurrection of Jesus, Küng argues, does not require an empty tomb; his personal identity could be preserved without the corpse being transformed and taken up into his new, 'spiritual' existence. To an almost painful degree, Thomas Aquinas and other medieval theologians often took a similar tack in arguing from principles (whether real or merely alleged) to facts. Both in the medieval past and today, however, it would seem to me much sounder to establish and accept facts and then try to make sense of them, rather than begin with general principles, in this case principles about continuity between something we know by experience (our earthly existence) and something of which we have no direct experience ('heavenly' existence).

What kind of a case can be made for the particular fact in question — namely, Jesus' empty tomb? Then we can ask: If we accept the historical fact of the empty tomb, what could it mean theologically?

As regards the fate of Jesus' body, both the tradition behind the Synoptic Gospels (Matthew, Mark and Luke) and that which entered John's Gospel testified to one (Mary Magdalene) or more women finding Jesus' grave to be open and empty. Early polemic against the message of his resurrection supposed that the tomb was known to be empty. Naturally the opponents of the

Christian movement explained away the missing body as a plain case of theft (Matthew 28:11–15). But we have no early evidence that anyone, either Christian or non-Christian, ever alleged that Jesus' tomb still contained his remains. Furthermore, the place of women in the story of the empty tomb speaks for its historical authenticity. If this story had been a legend created by early Christians, they would have attributed the discovery of the empty tomb to male disciples rather than women, who in that culture did not count as valid witnesses. Legend-makers do not usually invent positively unhelpful and counterproductive material.

If we are satisfied about the historical case for the empty tomb, the further challenge then is to explore and appreciate what this discovery could and does mean. How would it improve our Easter faith and theology if we understood something of the empty tomb's significance?

First of all, the emptiness of Jesus' grave reflects the holiness of what it once held, the corpse of the incarnate Son of God who lived for others and died to bring a new covenant of love for all people. This 'Holy One' could not 'see corruption' (Acts 2:27). Secondly, the very emptiness of the tomb can suggest and symbolise the fullness of the new and everlasting life into which Jesus has gone. Thirdly, the empty tomb expresses something vital about the nature of redemption — that redemption is much more than a mere escape from our scene of suffering and death. Rather it means the transformation of this material, bodily world with its whole history of sin and suffering. The first Easter began the work of finally bringing our universe home to its ultimate destiny. God did not discard Jesus' earthly corpse, but mysteriously raised and transfigured it so as to reveal what lies ahead for human beings and their world. In short, that empty tomb in Jerusalem is God's radical sign that redemption is not an escape to a better world but an extraordinary transformation of this world.

2. Faith

The discussion of some serious and frivolous historical challenges, which a contemporary Easter Christology may have to face, has brought me to matters of faith and theology. Once again I want to sample a few questions to exemplify what such a Christology will need to come to terms with.

A Christology centred on Easter will not amount to much nowadays unless it offers some tests for verifying belief in Jesus as risen from the dead. While granting the essential roles of divine grace and human freedom, can we in any way establish the reasonableness of Easter faith? What public checks and other evidence are available for accepting Christ's resurrection and knowing it to have truly happened? So long as a Christology does not provide any help in justifying Easter faith, one may find that theologising about the resurrection will lack a basic credibility.

A cumulative set of checks for justifying and validating faith would raise *historical* questions about the origins of Christianity (Did Jesus appear to his disciples? Was his tomb found to be empty?) and about the story of the Christian church (What testable and valuable differences has belief in the resurrection made to human life?). Tests should also move to the area of direct, *personal experience*. Does faith in the resurrection successfully re-order my sense of the world and offer me deep and permanent satisfaction through living by its light? This check recognises that the apostolic testimony to Christ's rising from the dead will prove credible if that resurrection somehow rings true in my personal experience and is confirmed by it.

In short, I propose that tests for verifying Christ's resurrection will be both public and personal. Some tests will raise questions that are more historical and 'from the outside'. Other checks will look for favourable evidence 'from the inside', in the ways that resurrection belief correlates 'existentially' with the individual's personal experience.

John's Gospel clearly suggests ways in which the truth of the risen Christ is not only legitimated through historical witness from the past (19:35; 20:30 f; 21:24), but also proves itself in the practice of life. As we saw above in Chapter 2, Jesus invites people to let him join them in interpreting and dealing with various profound and troubling experiences. He interprets and heals religious doubt for Nicodemus (3:1–21; 7:50 f; 19:39), marital breakdowns for the Samaritan woman (4:4–42), a serious sickness for the royal official (4:46–53), their brother's death for Martha and Mary (11:1–44) and a terrible personal failure for Simon Peter (21:15–19). In such typical human experiences, faith in the risen Christ can validate itself in practice.

Last Easter a group of my friends spent two weeks in the People's Republic of China. A question put to them by their guide pointed to the need to justify not only historically but also experientially the living presence of the risen Christ: 'How does Jesus Christ function for you today?'

3. Theology

In *The Easter Jesus* (London, 1973), I approached Christ's resurrection from the standpoint of history, faith and theology. That triple division still looks appropriate. Let me complete this chapter by mentioning briefly three theological issues that could be treated in a Christology built around the events of Good Friday and Easter Sunday. The three issues concern, respectively, the dialogue with Asian religions, the Christological dimension of liberation theology, and a question that emerges from recent British theology.

When interpreting and communicating Christ with the great religions of Asia, some Christian writers move straight from the historical Jesus to the cosmic Logos. In doing so, they omit something utterly essential. Let me explain. On the one hand, in his earthly story Jesus lived a particular, limited life. How can such a small piece of

50

human history possess absolute and decisive value for all men and women of all times, places and cultures? On the other hand, the Logos theology of some Greek fathers that has been revived in recent years lacks specificity. The notion of the Word or Wisdom through which the universe was formed and exists picks up a theme of extremely wide religious appeal. But to acknowledge a divine Logos manifested in the orderly structure of the cosmos does little as such for the Christian dialogue with Buddhism and Hinduism. By itself that truth is too general.

What links the specific history of Jesus with the general truth of the eternal Logos is the event of the resurrection. Through that event a particular human life not only was seen to have had but also assumed universal and absolute importance. In the words of Peter's address on the day of Pentecost, 'Let all the house of Israel therefore know assuredly that God has made him both Lord and Christ, this Jesus whom you crucified' (Acts 2:36). It is the resurrection that effectively shows that the specific, limited story of Jesus was in fact the earthly history of the eternal Logos. The risen, 'post-existent' Son of God (Romans 1:3 f) was and is identical with the pre-existent Son sent into the world (Galatians 4:4), the 'beloved Son' in and through whom 'all things were created' (Colossians 1:13, 16), the Word who in the beginning 'was with God' (John 1:1). In rising from the dead Jesus became effective Saviour and Lord for all the nations (symbolically represented by the mixed crowd Peter addresses at Pentecost).[10]

Second, to judge from the Vatican's 'Instruction on Certain Aspects of the "Theology of Liberation" ' (from the Congregation for the Doctrine of the Faith, 6 August 1984), nothing much about the resurrection comes into view from theologies of liberation. In both its positive and negative reactions to that movement, the document never mentions the resurrection of the crucified Jesus.

It is not that liberation theologies simply fail to discuss the Easter mystery. Leonardo Boff notes that through the resurrection the whole 'human reality' of Jesus enters a 'situation' of final, universal influence. Without the resurrection 'there would be no Christ — only the prophet of Nazareth, in the line of the great religious innovators in human history'.[11] Hugo Assmann reflects on what the risen Christ's active power entails today across the face of human history.

To affirm in faith the actuating presence of the power of Christ means to struggle in history where defeat is but preparing the way for victory, to struggle in the ongoing process of liberation, in the presence of the ongoing dialectic of cross and resurrection today.[12]

Faced with debate about ontological and functional language in Christology, Lamberto Schuurman emphasises a universal, functional result of Jesus' resurrection — the invitation to discipleship.

. . . it [the resurrection] should be interpreted first of all as the universal appropriation of the historical Jesus' functional program. Viewed in this way the resurrection will not invite us to a metaphysical contemplation but to discipleship, to getting the program of the historical Jesus underway in new situations.[13]

Jon Sobrino wishes to understand and interpret the resurrection through the search for justice in a history of human suffering: 'Basic discussion about Jesus' resurrection . . . has to do with the triumph of justice. Who will be victorious, the oppressor or the oppressed?' (*Christology at the Crossroads*, Maryknoll, 1978, p. 244).

Nevertheless, the Vatican document of late 1984 faithfully, if perhaps inadvertently, reflects a feature of liberation theologies. They inevitably underplay the full significance of the resurrection because they are often bent on developing Christologies on the basis of Jesus' ministry and death. Sobrino, for example, takes as the starting-point and centre of Christology 'the person, proclamation, activity, attitudes, and death by crucifixion of Jesus of Nazareth insofar as all of this can be gathered from the New Testament texts' (*ibid*. p. 351).

In Chapter 2 of this book I have already argued for the paschal mystery as the appropriate focus of Christology. In the second edition of *What are they saying about Jesus?* (Ramsey, 1983) I assembled some reasons for disagreeing with Sobrino's choice and maintaining the Christological centrality of the paschal mystery (pp. 54–6). Here one point can be added. Liberation theologies are deeply concerned with issues of justice and injustice. Their Christologies would be greatly enriched if they reflected more on a major aspect of Jesus' resurrection from the dead: the full and final justice it promises to the poor and oppressed. Of course, that theme is not totally missing in the work of Sobrino and other liberation theologians. Nevertheless, they cannot develop it adequately, since in general they fail to focus very much on the resurrection.

A last requirement for an Easter Christology comes from a question that has repeatedly surfaced in recent British theology. If one recognises in Jesus' resurrection an 'act of God', what is the meaning and truth of such divine interventions in the 'ordinary' course of human history? How do we understand and interpret such special activities of God in our midst? The issue extends beyond the resurrection to such matters as the role of God in Israel's history, the event of the incarnation, the writing of inspired Scriptures and episodes of special grace in the lives of believers. All the same, the event of the resurrection forms the climactic case of such divine interventions. What sense, then, can give claims about the divine activity involved in raising Jesus from the dead and thus inaugurating the end of all history? Sooner or later this task must be tackled by anyone who develops a Christology around the paschal mystery.

5
SAVIOUR
AND
EMMANUEL

Of this book, as can often happen elsewhere, one might say, 'In its beginning was its end.' When handling the human condition, Chapter 1 remarked on the frequent and proper link made between what Jesus Christ has done for us (soteriology) and who he is in himself (Christology). This concluding chapter takes up those two themes to propose some lines for thought.

1. Jesus as Saviour

Any serious and systematic reflection on Jesus Christ must obviously offer something about his saving or redeeming function. At the same time, no account of redemption will amount to much unless and until it says something about the evil from which Christ saves and will save us. The knowledge of his goodness as redeemer is essentially linked to a knowledge of evil and suffering.

What shape do suffering, sin and evil assume in our world? Clearly there is no short or easy answer to that question, even if I were to limit myself to asking: What is evil in Australia? In Chapter 1 I nominated death, absurdity and hatred as constituting a triple typology that allows us to classify our experiences of evil and suffering. Here I want to outline another triple typology (greed, fear and fatalism), which could also prove serviceable in making sense of what we hope to be saved and liberated from.

(a) Greed

Around the world few modern phenomena symbolise human greed more powerfully than organised crime, both national and international. By the way it accumulates money and power, organised crime has corrupted many communities and even national governments. It has generated new levels of violence and made it impossible for millions of people to exercise freely their basic civil liberties.

Organised crime symbolises shockingly the terrible effects of unchecked greed. But public life and recent history yield innumerable other examples of the evil caused by human greed. The arms industry yields spectacular profits, but the citizens of a country and their neighbours must often pay a terrible price for 'military hardware'. Around the world the standards of wealth claimed by majorities or even dominant minorities can put a dignified and free existence simply out of reach for whole groups of people. I think here of what my predecessors, the European settlers in Australia, did to the Aborigines whose land rights were violated in the interests of sheep, wheat, cattle and mining. As so often, justice fell and continues to fall before the passion for gold, uranium and bauxite.

Add, too, the havoc caused in married life and family life by greed for possessions and affection. Over and over again fidelity to one's spouse and children gets crowded out by excuses for a destructive affair ('I feel lonely and she needs me'). Squabbles over money can tear families asunder. In private life, no less than in public affairs, greed proves itself corrupting and destructive.

(b) Fear

In the late twentieth century the world must witness the insane lengths to which fear can drive the two superpowers. Over 50,000 nuclear warheads not only threaten the Russian and American people with mutually assured destruction, but could also end the human story. A *graffito* I saw recently on a wall in Rome pleads, 'Don't fire at the planet (*Non sparate al pianeta*).' But our world leaders might well do so. Fear could drive them to prefer national defence over human survival. In the meantime we must all go on living perpetually on the edge of extinction.

The evil effects of this international reign of fear are innumerable. Let me mention just one local example. In 1946 a rocket and atomic-weapon proving range was established at Woomera in South Australia. Patrol officers for the Weapons Research Establishment 'trucked in' the Pintupi and other Aboriginal groups to settlement points. What happened on the Woomera Range was part of a wider pressure brought to bear right down to the 1960s. To clear the desert for military tests or sometimes simply to suit the convenience of white officials, Aborigines were forced to leave their ancestral lands for centralised settlements in other areas.

Such international and national examples write large what occurs so often at the personal level. Fear seems to describe precisely what dominates countless lives. People can live in fear of losing their job, growing old, meeting the sick and the young, being punished by God, being rebuffed by a relative or friend, being criticised by their neighbours, contracting some incurable disease and facing death. Sometimes the fears remain faceless and make up a kind of primordial anxiety that haunts and even controls our existence. Whatever form it takes, fear often drives human beings to disregard callously the rights and needs of others. It can warp and twist one's own life into a painful mess.

(c) Fatalism

One enemy that liberation theologians have been concerned to exorcise is fatalism, that passive resignation that has led millions of poor and oppressed people to accept their bondage. So far from following a Jesus who can inspire and help them to be delivered from their deadly situation, they have often worshipped him as one who comforts them in their futile and meaningless sufferings.

Once again an international evil (in this case some aspects of Latin American history) writes large what we find in innumerable lives around the world. No matter what they hope to achieve and even manage to do, people can finish up interpreting their story fatalistically: a desolate march into middle age and beyond it to the final failure of death. Seen in these terms, life turns into an evil to be endured rather than a blessing to be lived. In effect, such people answer 'No' to those *graffiti* from Northern Ireland: 'Is there life after birth? Is there life before death?'

Personally I have often wondered how much latent fatalism haunts the consciousness of my own country. For five years I lived just a few hundred yards from the monument in Royal Park (Melbourne) marking the place from which the disastrous Burke and Wills expedition started in 1860. Why is it that Australians seem to pass over successful nineteenth-century explorers such as Thomas Mitchell and John McDougall Stuart and cherish rather the memory of futile failures like Robert O'Hara Burke and William Wills, who perished in the centre of the continent, or Ludwig Leichhardt, who disappeared in the desert? Australian fiction often transmits the same sense of fatalism — from a pioneer woman's suffering expressed in Henry Lawson's 1892 short story 'The Drover's Wife' to Thomas Keneally's *The Chant of Jimmie Blacksmith*. In that novel a young Aborigine strikes out violently against his oppressors, only to be caught, tried and hanged by a butcher. Nothing is saved, no one is redeemed.

The triad of greed, fear and fatalism, I suggest, may help to give a face to those deadly forces that oppress us and from which we need to be delivered. Certainly ever so much more should be said. *How*, for example, does Christ save us from this tyranny? All the same, the first thing that requires attention is those features of our actual human condition that call for liberation and healing. The triad of greed, fear and fatalism gathers up much of what keeps us in evil bondage.

(d) Power in Failure.

Fatalism invites a last comment before I move to the second half of this chapter. Faced with a tragic failure, we easily slip into a mood of empty resignation: 'It's not worth trying. That's the way things always end up.'

In the introduction to Book II of his *Republic* Plato long ago suggested the kind of fate that a perfectly just man could expect:

The just man, then, as we have pictured him, will be scourged, tortured, and imprisoned. His eyes will be put out, and after enduring every humiliation he will be crucified.

Some Fathers of the Church found this to be a remarkable, pagan prophecy of what happened to Jesus himself. Some Christians I know remark on the fact that Jesus was not merely a perfectly just man, but also a perfectly loving man. But then they add: 'See what came of him. They wiped him out so quickly. If you live the way Jesus did, you only end up like him a failure on a cross.'

Beyond question, failure can be viewed fatalistically. Yet something greater may be glimpsed there, a power and a promise that far exceed what was lost. Even the 'useless' deaths of incompetent explorers may yield a hint of this. So too does the story of Patsy Adam-Smith, a woman who left home in the 1950s to sail on little tramp steamers in the wild waters off Southern Australia.

Seven ships sank in . . . the six years I was at sea, including the two wooden vessels I sailed on and two whose crews we knew and searched for but never saw again . . .

I still grieve for those . . . shipmates, still weep for George MacCarthy, that noble buccaneer whose last words we heard on our ship's radio through the wind that was keening his passing. He stood alone on his sinking, storm-beaten, wallowing vessel.

'She answers the helm no more.' A little later: 'The sea has her now.' The shore station in Melbourne called over and over, 'Come in Willwatch. Come in Willwatch.' But we never heard his voice again. Nor those of his five crew he had earlier put over the side.[1]

Common sense can make little of the fate of MacCarthy and his men. But where courage takes men and women beyond the point where greed and fear would tell them to stay, an apparently futile death may speak of a loss that is neither absolute nor final. The loser may, after all, find life.

During the Spanish-American War of 1898, Henry Lawson wrote a poem celebrating the sense of honour that drove men to fight and die in a hopeless cause. I quote 'Dons of Spain' in full; it celebrates a holy 'madness' that no death can destroy.

> The Eagle screams at the beck of Trade; so Spain, as the
> world goes round,
> Must wrest the right to live or die from the sons of the
> land she found;
> For, as in the days when the buccaneer was abroad on
> the Spanish Main,
> The national honour's the thing most dear to the heart
> of the Dons of Spain.
>
> She had slaughtered thousands with fire and sword, as
> the Christian world doth know;
> We murder millions — but, thank the Lord! we only
> starve 'em slow.
>
> The times have changed since the days of old, but the
> same old rules obtain;
> We fight for Freedom, and God, and Gold, and the
> Spaniards fight for Spain.

We fought with the strength of moral right, but they, as
their ships went down,
Fought on because they were fighting-men — and their
armour helped them drown.
It mattered little what chance or hope, for ever the path
was plain;
The Church was the Church, and the Pope the Pope —
but the Spaniards fought for Spain.

Their Yankee foes may be kin to us (we are English,
heart and soul),
And proud of their national righteousness, and proud of
the lands they stole;
But we yet might pause while those brave men die, and
the death-pledge drink again —
For the sake of the past, if you're doomed, say I, may
your end be a grand one, Spain!

Then here's to the bravest of Freedom's foes that ever
with death have stood,
To the men with the courage to die on steel as their
fathers died on wood;
And here's a cheer for the flag unfurled in a hopeless
cause again,
For the sake of the days when the Christian world was
saved by the Dons of Spain.

Here and there in our history, literature and personal
experience, all of us will find enough to create a vision
of the kind of tragic failure that does not encourage
fatalistic resignation, but somehow promises something
new and greater — an Easter Sunday already vaguely
glimpsed even on Good Friday itself. If we succeed in
doing so, those life-giving failures will yield some sense
of what salvation through crucifixion might mean.
Through the vulnerability and failure of Calvary came
God's power to redeem and heal (2 Corinthians 12:9;
13:4).

2. Emmanuel

Some years ago a friend of mine was complaining about what he took to be the decline and fall of Roman Catholicism in France. His voice faltered as he summed things up: 'The French went in for Catholic Action. Then they pushed the line of *témoignage*, witness. Now they are satisfied with mere presence.'

At the time I wondered whether my friend was right in being disenchanted with the move from action to witness, and from witness to presence. I put it to myself this way: 'When I come to die, no one will be able to do anything for me, and I won't want anyone preaching to me. But I will certainly be reassured by the presence of a relative or friend.' Nowadays I wonder whether, inadvertently, my friend had stumbled on a good way of expressing the move from creation, through the history of Israel, on to the coming of Jesus Christ. God acted in creation. Moses and the prophets witnessed to the people. But Jesus Christ was God's personal presence among us.

Matthew calls Jesus 'Emmanuel, which means, God with us' (1:25; see 28:20). John's prologue climaxes with the announcement: 'The Word became flesh and dwelt among us' (1:14). This presence came about through the free love of God: 'In this was the love of God made manifest among us, that God sent his only Son into the world that we might live through him' (1 John 4:9).

Thinking of Jesus Christ in terms of divine presence carries several advantages. First, it looks back to God's special presence to the chosen people. The Israelites appreciated profoundly that blessing: 'What great nation is there that has a god so near to it as the Lord our God is to us, whenever we call upon him?' (Deuteronomy 4:7). Second, such an approach grasps a central theme of Jesus' ministry as reported by the Synoptic Gospels. Seized by his Father's presence, Jesus preached the nearness of the divine power and mercy: 'The time is fulfilled, and the kingdom of God is at hand; repent, and believe in the gospel' (Mark 1:15). Jesus' personal activity brought the divine presence to bear powerfully on people suffering from the forces of evil. In his words from Luke's Gospel: 'If it is by the finger of God that I cast out demons, then the kingdom of God has come upon you' (11:20).

Third, the notion of new forms of presence covers some important aspects of Jesus' resurrection. For example, his dialogue with the Father has been interrupted by death, but now it can be resumed in a full and final way. Through such language as 'sitting at the right hand of the Father' (Hebrews 1:3; Mark 16:19) and 'living to God' (Romans 6:10), the New Testament expresses the new presence between the risen Jesus and his Father. Easter brings a new presence between the risen Lord and the Holy Spirit. In his earthly life Jesus was driven by the Spirit (Mark 1:12) and worked 'in the power of the Spirit' (Luke 4:14). The new post-resurrection closeness allows Paul to say, 'The Lord is the Spirit' (2 Corinthians 3:17). The Spirit of the risen Lord also now works with new power in and through believers (Romans 5:5; 8:26; Galatians 4:6). Through faith and baptism they are inserted 'in Christ' (for example, Romans 8:1; 16:7; 1 Corinthians 15:22) and enjoy an intimate communion of life with him. His risen presence creates the new community of those who know him when they meet to pray in the Spirit (1 Corinthians 12:3), to read and hear the Scriptures (Luke 24:27, 32) and to celebrate the sacraments.

Rudolf Otto's account of God's holiness remains the classic version: *mysterium tremendum et fascinans*, the frightening and fascinating mystery. As risen from the dead, Jesus effectively reveals his divine sovereignty. The seer in the Book of Revelation conveys a sense of Jesus' new, mysterious presence, a presence both frightening and fascinating.

When I saw him, I fell at his feet as though dead. But he laid his right hand upon me, saying, 'Fear not, I am the first and the last, and the living one; I died, and behold I am alive for evermore . . . (Revelation 1:17–18).

Modifying Otto's formula to read 'a frightening and fascinating presence' catches up much of the feeling engendered by the risen Christ in and through the pages of Revelation. In the end, of course, one prays for that presence to be fully realised and disclosed: 'Come, Lord Jesus' (Revelation 22:20)

Furthermore, a Christology of presence points to two great challenges in the life of the Church. Over and over again saints such as Francis of Assisi and movements such as the theology of liberation have called on believers to grasp the fact of the Lord's special and privileged presence among the poor and the suffering. Jesus' words about the last judgement (Matthew 25:31–46) must always be carried further. They remain beautifully open-ended:

I was a Vietnamese refugee, and you gave me a chance.

I was an illegitimate and handicapped child, and you opened to me your home.

I was an underpaid and badly-housed Aborigine, and you tried to get me justice.

I mattered to no one and was about to take my life, when I felt the power of your concern and compassion.

Jesus' solidarity with sufferers extends beyond individuals to whole groups of persons: for example, the Jewish people, whose sufferings reached an unspeakable climax in our century. For Christian believers, the genocidal horror of the Holocaust also included the fact that it was an attempt to rid the world of a living sign of Jesus' presence. More than ever before, that sign that is the suffering Jewish people expressed the Jesus who continues to be in agony among us.

Take another group of people that have been deeply wronged, impoverished and persecuted, the Australian Aborigines. They have suffered and continue to suffer in the areas of health, housing, education, employment, land rights and other legal rights. They too are a sign of the Jesus who remains in agony among us.

A Christology that takes shape around the risen presence of the crucified Jesus may be better able than some other Christologies to meet the greatest pastoral challenge — how to mediate Jesus and his presence. At times the language of Christology still sounds like an attempt to avoid the reality of Jesus' presence and to avoid mediating that presence. I think here of some who stress in season and out the Council of Chalcedon's teaching on Christ's person in two natures. Those champions of Chalcedon may be perfectly orthodox, but the last thing their work manages to do is mediate the living presence of Jesus Christ.

In Matthew's opening chapter the angel of the Lord not only speaks of 'Emmanuel', but also reveals to Joseph the name Mary's son is to bear: 'You shall call his name Jesus, for he will save his people from their sins' (1:21). Two things take my attention here. First, the link between personal identity and function. Mary's son is Emmanuel, 'God-with-us'; he will function to save us from sin and evil. We might draw together these functional (or soteriological) and ontological aspects by talking of the saving divine presence of Jesus.

Second, Matthew reports and explains the name which Mary's son was given, Jesus. At times some who write Christologies think that name is best left alone. Or at least they go for many pages without using the name of Jesus. That tendency belongs to a more abstract style of Christology, one which is content to be less than fully historical and fails to unite who Jesus is as Son of God with what he does as Saviour of the world. Luke, presumably, would not be happy with any failure to name Jesus: 'There is no other name under heaven given among men by which we must be saved' (Acts 4:12).

It is worth noting, incidentally, a reluctance to use the name of Jesus on the part of many extreme traditionalists and their critics. To judge them at least by their public utterances, the supporters and many opponents of Archbishop Marcel Lefebvre talked easily about God, the Church, the Pope, the Mass and ecumenical councils. But frequently they appeared and still appear reluctant to invoke the name of Jesus.

In the second half of this chapter I set out to do only one thing: suggest how my friend's scheme of action, witness and presence could, quite beyond his original intentions, turn out to provide an attractive way of reflecting on Jesus, the one who was and remains God's personal presence among us.

EPILOGUE

This book has attempted to pour a little new wine into the bottle of Christology. These days, as Robert Schreiter indicates in *Constructing Local Theologies* (Maryknoll, 1985), the new wine must partly come from the vineyard of local Christologies. Like John's Gospel, such an approach will tell the story of Jesus together with our own. It will weave together the biblical narrative with the narratives of particular cultures, communities and individuals.

This epilogue adds some further thoughts and questions to the material and project treated in Chapter 3, the formation of a local Christology. But first, two clarifications on Chapter 1 and 2, respectively.

Chapter 1 noted three components for any adequate Christology: philosophy, history and eschatology. At the risk of oversimplifying matters, one could usefully propose that philosophy deals mainly with the present, history with the past and eschatology with the future. Philosophy focuses on general truths, history on particular persons and events, and eschatology on the final end of all things.

Symbolism figured among the topics discussed in Chapter 2. Symbols are the lifeblood of the real, interpersonal communication that binds believers together. They provide the medium in which faith and theology can survive. It would be worth taking up the questions: Where and how do we find a few unifying symbols for Christianity? Where and how can we find a few powerful symbols of Christ?

Chapter 3 could have tackled local Christological possibilities not only historically but also more theologically and anthropologically. Who and what is God in Australia? Are there any distinctive ideas about God available in the South Pacific? Who is *homo australis*? Do Australians have any particular slants on the human condition? Could their sense of national identity contribute anything at all to interpreting and communicating today the real humanity of Jesus Christ?

One could also explore imaginatively the ideas about God and the human condition furnished by the original inhabitants of this island-continent, the Australian Aborigines. Like the native peoples of North and South America, the Aborigines had no contact whatsoever with the cultural and religious matrix of the Jewish-Christian religion. Asian, African and European influences affected the history of God's people in the Old Testament period and during the subsequent rise of Christianity. But there was no such input from the Americas and Australia. From time immemorial the Aborigines developed separately their own characteristic ideas about human life, the world, the divine mystery and the hereafter.

Chapter 3 ended by finding meaning in the great natural sign which fills the Australian sky on clear nights, the constellation of the Southern Cross. That constellation also symbolises suffering and the need to reflect on suffering. A refusal to think in depth on suffering leaves Christology unreal and theology barren. The chapter might have started by collecting and examining popular images of Christ in Australia. If 'Christ the Liberator' galvanises believers in Latin America, what image of Jesus could transform Australian Christianity and society?

Chapter 3 could have mentioned a classic work that

does supply two tragic heroes in the Australian setting, Patrick White's *Riders in the Chariot*. That novel brings together representatives of two suffering peoples, a Jewish refugee in an alien land (Mordecai Himmelfarb) and an Aborigine (Alf Dubbo). The climax of the book re-enacts the drama of Good Friday in the new society of post-World War II Australia. Himmelfarb is the crucified Christ-figure. Dubbo plays the role of Peter in this passion story. Chapter 3 also could have mentioned the classic Australian hero, Ned Kelly. Sydney Nolan and other artists and writers have articulated some Christological possibilities in the story and mythology of that outlaw.

This book has lined up some of the agenda for a contemporary Christology and made proposals for a local-style approach. It hopes to initiate a conversation. Like the lectures on which it was based, this book aims to leave to its readers the very considerable work that has still to be done.

NOTES

Chapter 1

1. See, for example, Karl Rahner's 'Christology within an Evolutionary View of the World', *Theological Investigations 5*, pp. 157–92.

2. Edinburgh, 1928, p. 52.

Chapter 4

1. Thiering's *The Qumran Origins of the Christian Church* (Sydney, 1983) teems with assertions that are simply not supported by any evidence. Somehow she knows that Pilate's wife was involved in the religion of the Temple Scroll and that Judas Iscariot had pretended to share in the outlook of the Essenes (p. 215). By surrendering himself to Pilate (*ibid.*), Judas had in effect 'hanged himself' (Matthew 27:5) and is to be identified with the criminal who asked for Jesus' help (Luke 23:39–43) (p. 217). Thiering asserts that when John writes 'city' (19:20) he means the Qumran monastery. Without proof, she identifies Simon of Cyrene with the high priest Ananias of Qumran (p. 216). When Mark 14:36 reports Jesus praying 'Father, remove this cup from me', she turns this into an order from a certain Jonathan: if the need arose, Jesus was to die with dignity by accepting a cup of poison. On the cross, Jesus at first refused to drink the poison, *cholé* (Matthew 27:34)

(p. 217). Here Thiering slides over the fact that *cholé* means gall, not poison, and presses on to harmonise in her own extraordinary fashion the four passion narratives. The cry 'I thirst' (John 19:28) suggests that when the pain grew intolerable, Jesus cried out that he was now ready to drink the poison (*ibid.*).

At this point Thiering goes even further with assertions for which she can offer no evidence whatsoever: 'A decision was made [by whom?] to change the method of execution, and bury the three men alive in the tomb.' The soldiers 'saw that he [Jesus] was spiritually dead' and 'took him to be physically dead' (p. 218). Once Jesus, Simon Magus and Judas Iscariot were placed in the tomb, 'Simon worked quickly, despite his broken legs. He squeezed the juice from the aloes and poured it with the myrrh down the throat of Jesus. The poison that was not yet absorbed was expelled, and by 3 a.m. [Why not 2 a.m.? Or 6 a.m.?] it was known that he would survive' (p. 219). Thiering's further 'reconstruction' of the order of events is just as full of items that would be hilariously funny if they were not so solemnly meant. The two angels whom Mary Magdalene saw in the tomb (John 20:12) were in fact Simon Magus and Judas (p. 220). After his remarkably lucky escape from death, Jesus remained with his followers until the end of the history recorded in the Book of Acts (p. 225). At one point he crossed to Europe with Luke; the 'we' passages in Acts always indicate the presence of the two of them (p. 226).

Thiering's version of the 'swoon theory' rests on gratuitous assertions, misinterpreted evidence and the decision to line up forcibly the Gospel material with the Qumran documents.

I much prefer the version of the Irish novelist George Moore (1852-1933). In his *The Brook Kerith: a Syrian story* (New York, 1916) Jesus is 'a pious Essene' (p. ix), a 'rough shepherd philosopher' (p. x), whose fate runs as follows:

The man is put on the cross and is lifted from it apparently dead, but he is not dead, and when he wakens from his swoon he perceives that he was mistaken in all things: angels did not come down from Heaven to lift him from the cross and bear him back to his father, and the world still subsists the same as before (p. ix).

After he revives in the tomb (chapter XVIII), Joseph of Arimathea carries him out. Jesus recovers and his activity continues almost to the end of the book, when he and Paul part company (chapter XLI). Whatever one says about Moore's 'evidence', *The Brook Kerith* is a much better read than *The Qumran Origins of the Christian Church*.

2. *A New Life of Jesus* (London, 1879), 1, p. 412.

3. Graves and Podro gave this title to their book because they claimed that Jesus visited Rome in the late forties.

4. See my *The Easter Jesus* (London, rev. ed., 1980) pp. 30–2.

5. See my 'Luminous Appearances of the Risen Christ', *Catholic Biblical Quarterly* 46 (1984) pp. 247–54.

6. 'La Genèse de la foi en la résurrection de Jésus: une nouvelle tentative', *La Pâque du Christ: mystère de salut*, ed. M. Benzerath et al., Lectio Divina 112 (Paris, 1982) pp. 51–74, especially at pp. 64–70. (This piece also appeared as 'Zur Entstehung des Glaubens an die Auferstehung. Ein neuer Versuch', *Freiburger Zeitshrift für Philosophie und Theologie* 30 (1983) pp. 73–98.)

7. *Ibid.* p. 70. Incidentally, in dealing with these texts from Mark, I simply want to note the absence of any reference to post-resurrection appearances, not to discuss their historical authenticity. (Did Jesus, for example, really predict his death and resurrection?)

8. See J. Kremer, 'Zur Diskussion über "das leere Grab"', *Resurrexit*, ed. E. Dhanis (Rome, 1970) p. 158, fn. 70.

9. *New Testament Studies* 31 (1985) pp. 39–67.

10. In the whole inter-religious dialogue Christians

have dwelt incessantly on the incarnation, while largely ignoring the resurrection of the crucified Jesus. Paul Knitter's *No Other Name?: a critical survey of Christian attitudes towards world religions* (Maryknoll, 1985) inadvertently testifies to this phenomenon. His report on the present state of the dialogue rarely mentions Jesus' resurrection.

11. 'Images of Jesus in Brazilian Liberal Christianity', *Faces of Jesus: Latin American Christologies*, ed. J. M. Bonino (Maryknoll, 1984) p. 25.

12. 'The Actuation of the Power of Christ in History', ibid. p. 136.

13. 'Christology in Latin America', ibid. p. 166.

Chapter 5

1. 'Vive la difference', *Age* (Melbourne) 19 January 1985.